PRAISE FOR JACKSON DEAN CHASE

— USA TODAY BESTSELLING AUTHOR —

AS SEEN IN
BUZZFEED AND THE HUFFINGTON POST

"[Jackson Dean Chase is] a fresh and powerful new voice."
— Terry Trueman, Printz Honor author of *Stuck in Neutral*

"[Chase] grabs readers from page one."
— Nate Philbrick, author of *The Little One*

"[Jackson Dean Chase] succeeds in taking fiction to a whole new level."
— TheBaynet.com

"[Jackson's fiction is] diligently crafted…"
— The Huffington Post

"Irresistible… [Jackson knows how to write] a heart-pounding story full of suspense, romance, and action!"
— Buzzfeed

MORE BOOKS BY JACKSON DEAN CHASE

NONFICTION

ULTIMATE AUTHOR'S GUIDE SERIES

#1 Writing Dynamite Story Hooks

#2 Writing Heroes & Villains

#3 Writing Monsters & Maniacs

#4 Writing Apocalypse & Survival

WRITERS' PHRASE BOOKS SERIES

#1 Horror Writers' Phrase Book

#2 Post-Apocalypse Writers' Phrase Book

#3 Action Writers' Phrase Book

#4 Fantasy Writers' Phrase Book

#5 Fiction Writers' Phrase Book (Series Sampler)

#6 Science Fiction Writers' Phrase Book

#7 Romance, Emotion, and Erotica Writers' Phrase Book

FICTION

BEYOND THE DOME SERIES

#1 Drone

#2 Warrior

#3 Elite

#4 Human

THE GODS WAR SERIES

#1 Titan

#2 Kingdom of the Dead

WRITING HEROES AND VILLAINS

A MASTERCLASS IN GENRE FICTION

JACKSON DEAN CHASE

JACKSON DEAN CHASE, INC.

First printing, June 2018

ISBN-13: 978-1721836390 / ISBN-10: 172183639X

Published by Jackson Dean Chase, Inc.

WRITING HEROES & VILLAINS

PUBLISHER'S NOTE

"...Nothing works if you don't have interesting characters and a good story to tell."

WRITING HEROES AND VILLAINS

PREFACE

WELCOME to *The Ultimate Author's Guide to Writing Heroes & Villains.*
This edition collects the first three volumes of my bestselling *How to Write Realistic Fiction* series, including quick start guides on *How to Write Realistic Characters, How to Write Realistic Men,* and *How to Write Realistic Women.* For this "ultimate" edition, I have revised and expanded them all.

This book is jam-packed with the essentials of how to write compelling heroes, villains, love interests, sidekicks, and teams, all the way down to the entire supporting cast and even those wacky minor characters that add so much spice to scenes.

It includes how to write anti-heroes, reluctant heroes, and catalyst heroes, plus templates for the heroic "everyman," tricksters, warriors, and characters with special powers (whether psychic, superhero, or supernatural).

Not only do I cover all that hero business, but I cover villains too: tempters, traitors, false mentors, and the rest of the rogues gallery we love to hate.

I also go into incredible, eye-opening detail about how to write realistic male and female characters. If you've ever struggled to write the opposite sex, then this book is for you. Not just hair, fashion, and makeup tips, either (although they're in here too), but real in-depth gender psychology. You'll learn the secret "rules" by which men and women operate: how they think and *why* they act the way they do.

I've broken the subjects up into three easy to read parts to help you find the information you need fast:

- Part 1: *How to Write Realistic Characters*
- Part 2: *How to Write Realistic Men*
- Part 3: *How to Write Realistic Women*

This is a book for anyone serious about the craft of writing fiction, comics, or screenplays. I've condensed all my years of study and practice into one fun, easy book, loaded with examples from your favorite TV, films, comics, and novels.

Come on in and take the ride!

— JACKSON DEAN CHASE
Get a free book at
www.JacksonDeanChase.com

HOW TO WRITE REALISTIC CHARACTERS

INTRODUCTION

"Things were easier for the old novelists... their heroes were good through and through, their villains wholly bad."

— W. SOMERSET MAUGHAM

TODAY'S READERS want complex, realistic characters that struggle as much as they succeed. I'm not just talking about external struggles, but internal ones. Characters can't be too good or too evil, but must possess some shades of gray. In short, they should seem real—and real people are flawed.

What about carefully constructed plots and world-building? Are having these enough to make up for a lack of realistic characters? No. All your plots and setting details won't mean a thing if readers don't care about your characters.

That's where this book comes in. By implementing the strategies you learn in this quick start guide, you will have an unbeatable system for creating the compelling characters your story deserves.

— JACKSON DEAN CHASE
Get a free book at www.JacksonDeanChase.com

THE DIFFERENCE BETWEEN PERFECT AND REALISTIC CHARACTERS

"Perfect heroines, like perfect heroes, aren't relatable, and if you can't put yourself in the protagonist's shoes, not only will they not inspire you, but the book will be pretty boring."

— CASSANDRA CLARE

EVERY HERO SHOULD BE LIKABLE in some way, or at least interesting. To do that, your hero needs to display some measure of wit and charm, as well as enough willpower to stand up to the villain. But heroes can't be perfect. They must be flawed, or risk becoming boring. That's the difference between Batman and Superman.

Batman's got all kinds of flaws, Superman's perfect. Which one sells more copies and puts more butts in seats? Batman. You can't fix perfect. It will always ring false to give Superman issues after he's already been established as perfect (and perfectly boring) for decades. Now if Batman overcomes a flaw, fans will be proud of him, but they won't get bored because they know he'll never be perfect, no matter how hard he tries.

Blowing up the Death Star or teaching an uptight town how to dance are all well and good. This outer journey is the main plot, the story arc that changes the world (or some small part of it). It's also the initial reason people buy into your story, but it's not what truly satisfies them. What they really want to see are heroes who struggle to change themselves in relation to their outer journey.

To do this, every hero needs an inner journey. They get one by facing down their flaws—this constitutes the character arc which makes up the emotional subplot. The success or failure of the character arc sets the tone for the story arc. Let me say that again:

The success or failure of the character arc sets the tone for the story arc.

It's the difference between the bittersweet tragedy of *Butch Cassidy and the Sundance Kid* and the joyful triumph of *Star Wars, Episode IV: A New Hope*. Butch and Sundance struggle to change and fail, so they must die (albeit in a blaze of glory). Luke Skywalker and Han Solo struggle to change and succeed, so they live and triumph and go on to have other adventures in a galaxy far, far away.

Note that "live or die" can simply mean "win or lose." Some losers get a second chance in the sequel. For example, Rocky Balboa loses the big boxing match to Apollo Creed at the end of *Rocky*, but beats him in *Rocky II*, and guess what? It's twice as satisfying for Rocky and the audience. If Rocky had failed to beat Creed a second time, the audience would have been justifiably angry at both Rocky and the screenwriter. The whole sequel would have been pointless!

That's not to say that you can't have a chronic "loser" continue his adventures (see The Catalyst Hero, below), but he must be a true underdog people can root for. And because he rarely changes (or needs to), that means he must change the lives of those he comes into contact with for the better. He helps others succeed at their story and character arcs, but ends up alone and riding off into the sunset at the end (as in *Mad Max: Fury Road*).

Eventually, this type of hero must complete his overarching story and character arc, and he should do so successfully. After all, he's suffered so long, he deserves it and the audience demands it. In most cases, this ends the series, so if you're not ready to end it, you should give your underdog glimmers of hope every so often instead—both to remind him and the audience what's at stake in the bigger picture.

While it's generally accepted wisdom that when the hero's inner journey fails, the outer one does too (and vice versa), that's not always the case. There are exceptions where succeeding at an inner journey could mean the hero no longer cares to succeed on his outer journey.

For example, consider the tough jock who passes his prom king crown to the lonely outcast because it means more to the outcast than it ever will to him. He's learned this the hard way over the course of the story, overcoming his arrogant jock flaws in the process. So by the end, he's not only willing to sacrifice outer success for inner success, he *must* do it, or he won't be able to live with himself.

The jock has changed and grown as a person, and so his original outer journey no longer holds meaning to him—but helping the outcast does, and that becomes his new one. The best part is this helps the outcast complete his inner and outer journey as well. The outcast no longer can fail to hide behind excuses of "nobody likes me" and "all jocks are jerks." If you've done your job right, and written the jock and outcast as realistic, flawed characters who we can empathize with, then you've written a winner.

A BRIEF OVERVIEW OF THREE-ACT STRUCTURE

"I believe in three-act structure. When I say that to novel people, or people in the world of books, they go, 'Well, that's a film thing.' However, even a good joke has three acts."

— STEPHEN J. CANNELL

THE HERO'S STORY and character arc can be broken down into a simple Three-Act Structure:

In Act 1, the hero is briefly seen living in her Ordinary World, and we learn she has a problem that needs fixing. This problem is usually invisible to the hero and must be pointed out by a member of the supporting cast, or sometimes a minor character. The hero does not know how to change at this point.

Regardless, an inciting incident (aka "the catalyst") occurs that forces the hero out of her Ordinary World. This could be a zombie invasion, losing her job, getting cancer, etc. The villain easily defeats her, but she stubbornly clings to the "safety" of her Ordinary World, not realizing the harder she fights, the more trouble she gets into.

Basically, as a writer, you need to keep asking yourself, "How can I make things worse for my hero?" That's what pushes her toward change, and also what determines the pace of the story. Too fast, and there is *not enough time* for her to properly reflect on changing. That will make the change feel forced and not credible. Too slow, and there is *too much time* for her to reflect and second-guess. Her change will seem snail-like and your story becomes boring.

In Act 2, the hero takes defensive actions to evade the villain until she reaches her breaking point. She must be made to see and confront that who she was is no longer who she is or wants to be. There is no turning back. She is becoming a new person now, with new skills, new allies, and new goals, but she is not all the way there yet.

This realization only happens *after* the villain attacks her and her allies harder than ever and she is defeated again. This signals the midpoint of the story. The hero emerges determined to change and grow into a person capable of defeating the villain.

(Note that in more literary, character-driven works, the "villain" could be addiction, mental illness, or some other inner demon, though it will have villainous physical manifestations via police, coworkers, doctors, lawyers, etc.)

In Act 3, the hero goes on the offensive. However, even though she wins some fights, this does not vanquish the villain—it only shows how insanely powerful he is. The hero is again defeated, coming close to death herself and/or losing someone close to her (often a mentor who is killed or love interest who is captured). She has reached an all-time low and contemplates suicide, surrender, or escape.

The villain seems invincible. But what the hero does not realize is that the confrontation has given her a valuable insight into how the villain can be defeated. This insight is something that should have been previously foreshadowed in the story, though it would not have been known to the hero or deemed important if it was. The insight could take the shape of an ability, ally, object, or information.

Rather than give in to despair, the hero decides to confront the villain one last time. By doing so, she proves she is no longer becoming a hero, but has become one. This gives her the courage and confidence she needs to recognize the valuable insight and formulate a clever plan to surprise the villain. There is hope now—real, not imagined. She gathers her allies and weapons, and using the insight, attacks the villain with everything she's got!

The simplest stories would let this play out to a predictable (and boring) happy ending, but I'm betting you don't want to settle for that. What should happen instead is the insight the hero is relying on proves to be only half-right, not enough, or plain wrong—perhaps even a trick.

However, if the insight is completely correct, then the villain has set up some deadly (and unexpected) obstacle to prevent the hero from exploiting his weakness.

In any event, the villain, realizing the danger he is in, takes immediate action to surprise, demoralize, and defeat the hero with everything he has. The hero and villain both take heavy losses, including the defeat of their allies (in ascending order, from weakest to strongest). But it's still not enough to stop the villain. It's time for the final showdown, the climax where the hero and villain face each other, one on one.

It is at this point the villain can't resist saying or doing something so gloating or hateful that it forces the hero to instantly resolve her inner journey one way or another.

If she fails to resolve her inner journey, the villain soundly defeats her and we have a tragic ending.

If she succeeds, she suddenly realizes what she must do—she must sacrifice (or be willing to sacrifice) everything she holds dear, including her own life, to defeat the villain. If the valuable insight to the villain's defeat was only half-right before, the other half falls into place now, and the hero is quick to act on it.

In his arrogance, the villain is unprepared or unwilling to believe the hero could ever beat him, and though he makes a last-ditch attempt to stop her, he cannot withstand her relentless, inspired assault. The villain is soundly defeated, the day is won, and the hero enjoys her happy ending.

That does not mean the villain (or the evil he represents) is gone forever, but it will take time for to rebuild, and the hero will be better prepared to fight next time.

This type of last minute "pop-up scare" or epilogue is common in horror stories, but can be relied upon whenever you have need of a strong, recurring villain or greater evil.

HERO ARCHETYPES

"In the film world, we can all be heroes. In the real world, where heroism can cost you your life or the life of the ones you love, people aren't so willing to make those sacrifices. When they do, they are set apart from the rest of us."

— JOHN RHYS-DAVIES

THERE ARE TWO MAIN HERO ARCHETYPES: Catalyst Heroes and Reluctant Heroes. Both offer their own set of challenges and rewards. Note that rival theories suggest there are at least eight, and as many as fifty-two archetypes. To me, that's not just confusing, it's overwhelming. What I've done is condense all that fancy talk down into the two main archetypes and six subtypes you find in popular novels, short stories, comic books, and screenplays. Rest assured, all of the fifty-two archetypes from other theories easily fit into my "bite-size" formula.

● The Catalyst Hero comes into your story fully formed. His role is not to change (well, not too much or too often), but rather to enact positive change in others. Series heroes are often catalysts. Think Captain America, James Bond, The Lone Ranger, or most any action hero. They are fearless, self-sacrificing exemplars of their type who rarely make mistakes they can't scheme or fight their way out of.

● Most catalyst heroes are respected and rewarded for doing good deeds, but not all. Some catalysts are deeply mistrusted and misunderstood, even persecuted and pursued (such as Kane in *Kung-Fu*, David Banner in *The Incredible Hulk*, or Richard Kimble in *The Fugitive*, which are pretty much all the same brilliant TV series).

Even if your catalyst hero is retired and presents himself as a reluctant hero, deep down, he's not. That's because of the speed with which he transitions back to his old heroic ways. He's already made the journey, and being a hero to him is just like riding a bicycle: he never forgot how to do it.

The benefit of the retired catalyst is you get to flirt with the reluctant hero tropes without having to do all the work. The retired catalyst's catch phrase is, "I'm getting too old for this," and maybe he grumbles a lot, but he's secretly pleased to be recognized and needed again. Retirement doesn't suit him, and he'd rather go out in a blaze of glory.

● Reluctant Heroes come into the story unwilling at first to take heroic action. Some may arrive already successful at one thing or another, while others will be unformed nobodies or even malformed minor villains. They may begin complacent, ignorant, naïve, arrogant, or selfish, but never irredeemably bad or broken. Think Frodo Baggins, Han Solo, Spider-Man, and Tyrion Lannister from *Game of Thrones*. None of them *wanted* to be heroes, but circumstances forced them to be... even if they went kicking and screaming (or drunk).

Reluctant heroes are punished for doing good deeds. All it takes is one spontaneous act of kindness or mercy to strip them of everything and change their destiny forever. This is especially true for minor villains who undergo a change of heart. They end up paying an unthinkable price for doing the right thing because they hang out with bigger villains who regard kindness as not only a weakness, but dangerous in their line of work.

The rewards reluctant heroes get for their deeds are small and personal at first. As they grow into full-fledged heroes (stumbling along the way), the rewards get bigger, but so do the risks.

Reluctant heroes can be the most satisfying to write and to watch, because they have an inner journey as well as an outer one. We see them change themselves for the better even as they enact positive change in others.

HERO SUBTYPES

"Heroes are ordinary people who make themselves extraordinary."

— GERARD WAY

THERE ARE SIX COMMON SUBTYPES OF HEROES: Three mundane (every-man, trickster, and warrior), and three special (psychic, superhero, and supernatural). The three specials are really just templates you layer over mundanes to give them more exciting powers. Each has different strengths and flaws.

EVERYMAN HERO

The Everyman (or Everywoman) is neither amazingly fast nor strong, and has no special powers. What he does have is a core set of beliefs and willingness to stand up to threats. He uses these (and an awful lot of willpower) to win the day. An everyman may also have a specialized skill set that helps him overcome problems, or simply a big heart and an open mind. He could be a nobody or somebody in his world: from privileged elite to the working class or even homeless.

The fragility of this hero often confines him to YA fiction, romance novels, dramas, horror, legal or medical thrillers, and more literary stories where he is not expected to confront (or survive) the sort of world-shattering villains Trickster, Warrior, and Special heroes must face.

That doesn't mean an everyman doesn't lead an interesting life or can't change the world—he just does it in a way that makes sense for him, and is commensurate with his position and abilities.

However, some Everyman heroes grow into Tricksters, Warriors, and/or Specials, usually via an origin story where they begin without any powers and slowly develop them over the course of the story. Occasionally, you will see this concept reversed, such as Superman learning to hide his powers to fit in as an alien living among humans.

EVERYMAN EXAMPLES: Ben Mears from *'Salem's Lot*, Karl Kolchak from *The Night Stalker*, Elizabeth Bennett from *Pride and Prejudice*, Frodo Baggins from *The Lord of the Rings*, Dr. Leonard "Bones" McCoy from *Star Trek*, and Vikka Raymer from my sci-fi action/thriller, *Drone*.

TRICKSTER HERO

Tricksters are fast and clever, but never as physically powerful as warriors. They rely on their wits and flexibility to win the day, which may cause them to underestimate warriors. Most wizards, thieves, spies, and businessmen fall into this category.

TRICKSTER EXAMPLES: Doctor Who, Sherlock Holmes, Captain Picard from *Star Trek: The Next Generation*, Gandalf and Legolas from *The Lord of the Rings*, Danny Ocean from *Ocean's Eleven*, Mr. Spock from *Star Trek*, Peter Quill ("Starlord") from *Guardians of the Galaxy*, and Jon Warlock from my urban fantasy thriller, *Warlock Rising*.

WARRIOR HERO

Warriors are physically powerful and/or strategic, but never as fast or clever as tricksters. They rely on brute force and sound tactics to win the day, which may cause them to underestimate tricksters.

WARRIOR EXAMPLES: Captain Kirk from *Star Trek*, Conan the Barbarian, John McClane from *Die Hard*, Gimli from *The Lord of the Rings*, Mack Bolan, The Punisher, and Andrus Eaves from my urban fantasy thriller, *Titan* (co-written with Daniel Mignault).

IMPORTANT

Both warriors and tricksters will often have one or more signature weapons, tactics, or ruses they favor, and that fans of the character will expect to see them use *at least once* per story. To prevent this from getting old, you should mix things up a bit, and follow a progression, if possible.

For example, in my bestselling *Beyond the Dome* science fiction series, Rylee Mersum is a spy and assassin with a cybernetic arm. Over the course of three books, we see her use her "robot arm" in new and exciting ways. In *Warrior*, she shows the arm has a retractable sword blade in it. She uses it to punch through metal and kill her enemies. In *Elite*, she reveals she can fire the sword blade to impale a target. In *Human*, she fires the sword blade to impale two targets attacking her down a narrow corridor. She also reveals she can detach the robot arm and control it via a neural implant in her skull.

With each new book, Rylee uses her robot arm in expected and unexpected ways. Because she is a paranoid, secretive anti-hero, she does not reveal to the rest of her team what all her abilities are the first time we meet her.

If Rylee had revealed more than one or two new uses for her robot arm in a single book, it would have seemed like I was cheating. So be careful what abilities you give your characters and how quickly you reveal them, but whatever you do, don't overdo it! Less is more.

BACKGROUND QUESTIONS

Regardless of whether your hero is an everyman, trickster, or warrior, you need to ask yourself the following questions about his background:

1. Why and where did your hero undergo his training?
2. Is he self-taught? If not, who was his mentor, and what is their relationship?
3. Did your hero undergo his training by choice, or was he forced to do it?
4. Does your hero work as a lone wolf, with a small team, as part of a larger organization he believes in, or is he on the run?

MUNDANE FLAWS

Being overly ambitious, arrogant, cowardly, disloyal or loyal (to the wrong people), driven, foolhardy, greedy, sarcastic, or selfish. Mundane heroes may be introverts or extroverts depending on their nature (for example, many computer hackers are introverts).

WARNING

Be careful creating hybrid trickster/warrior heroes. *A hero who is good at too many things is not only boring, but hard to find credible challenges for.* Which is not to say it can't be done, but you must give hybrid heroes extra flaws to make up for their extra strengths—not just one incredibly rare and stupid thing like kryptonite. For that reason, it may be better to create a hybrid everyman with a trickster or warrior. You can also do this by creating a hybrid of an everyman and one of the special subtypes below.

The superhero and urban fantasy genres excel at these hybrids, such as Spider-Man really being newspaper photographer, Peter Parker, and *True Blood* bar owner, Sam Merlotte, also being a shapeshifter. These characters may travel to other dimensions, but they live in the real world, including holding down real jobs and having the same annoying problems regular people do.

Sometimes, a better solution than a hybrid is to have your hero team up with his opposite. This not only replaces the need for your hero to excel in too many areas, but creates a ton of extra fun arising from their daily banter.

For example, in Fritz Lieber's fantasy classic, *Ill Met in Lankhmar*, Fafhrd (a sword-swinging warrior) teams up with the Gray Mouser (a thief and wizard trickster). Their strengths and weaknesses complement each other, allowing them to achieve things neither could on their own.

THE SPECIAL HERO (PSYCHIC, SUPERNATURAL, OR SUPERHERO TEMPLATES)

There must be some kind of backstory to explain your hero's powers, and you must also come up with a set of "rules" for what she can and can't do. Once you've set the rules in place, don't break them!

You might be able to *bend* the rules once or twice, but only with a clear, logical reason and only if there are extreme consequences for the hero as a result. It's also best if the situation cannot be repeated, otherwise readers will wonder why the hero just doesn't do it again.

Are your hero's special powers the result of a curse, gift, magical training, or mutation? Is it hereditary?

1. Is she self-taught (or even aware of her power)?
2. What kind of mentor taught (or will teach) her to embrace and develop her power? Then ask yourself:
3. Is the mentor human? If not, what is it and why is it here?
4. What are the mentor's ultimate goals, and is your hero aware or approving of them?
5. Does the mentor work alone, with a small team, or with a larger organization?
6. What is your hero's relationship like with her mentor?

PSYCHIC ABILITIES

Determine what type of abilities your hero has and if any other abilities exist in your world. Psychic Ability examples include:

- Empathy (reading emotions)
- Mediumship (communicating with spirits)
- Mind control
- Precognition (predicting the future)
- Psychometry (seeing the past by "reading" objects)
- Psychokinesis (aka telekinesis, moving objects)
- Pyrokinesis (creating/manipulating fire)
- Telepathy (mental communication, either one-way or two-way)

A psychic with more than one power should be better at one than the others, and her reliance on it should shape her personality and actions.

Because they live so much in their heads, psychics are often tricksters and introverts.

Examples: Allison Dubois from *Medium*, Sookie Stackhouse from *True Blood*, Lorraine Warren from *The Conjuring*, Professor Xavier from *X-Men*.

PSYCHIC FLAWS

Psychic powers are notoriously unreliable and not always accurate or able to be interpreted correctly. They may cause temporary or permanent mental or physical problems, as well as social issues. Some will not believe in the hero's gift, thus putting themselves (and potentially others) in danger when they fail to heed her warnings.

SUPERHEROES

Determine what type of superpower(s) your hero has, and what other kinds of powers (including the heroes and villains who use them) exist in your world.

1. Are superpowers regulated by the government?
2. Who knows his secret?
3. What happens if his secret identity is "outed"?
4. What civil and legal repercussions might he face?
5. Does the hero believe he has been chosen or otherwise gifted, or does he consider his powers a curse?
6. Does he believe he is superior to mundanes?

Super power examples include:

- Aquatic powers (Aquaman, Namor the Submariner)
- Armored bones or skin (Colossus, Wolverine)
- Animal powers (including claws, fangs, tail, wings)
- Energy projection (Cyclops, The Human Torch)
- Echolocation (Daredevil)
- Flight (without wings) (Superman)
- Immunity to energy weapons
- Immunity to mundane weapons (Superman)
- Invisibility (The Invisible Woman)
- Magnetism (Magneto)
- Mind control (Kilgrave from *Jessica Jones*)
- Shape- or size-shifting (Ant-Man, Mr. Fantastic)
- Superior intellect (Professor X)
- Superior senses (Spider-Man)
- Superior technology (Batman, Iron Man)
- Super strength (Superman, the Hulk, the Thing)
- Super speed (The Flash)
- Teleportation (Nightcrawler)

A superhero with more than one power should be better at one more than the rest, and his reliance on his "signature power" should shape his personality and actions.

Superheroes can be tricksters or warriors based on their powers. They may be introverts or extroverts. It could fun to play against type (a "Mind Master" who hates people).

SUPERHERO FLAWS

The most obvious is having a secret identity that imperils the hero and loved ones if revealed, or perhaps the powers are useless in certain situations (for example, Superman in the presence of kryptonite, or Green Lantern having no power over anything colored yellow), or else the hero's quest to help others forces him to miss out on opportunities to help himself (such as Spider-Man).

SUPERNATURAL HEROES

Determine what type of supernatural creature or character your hero is and/or what type of magic they know (if any), and what other kinds of creatures and/or magic exist in your world.

Common examples include:

- Corporeal Undead (vampires, zombies, etc.)
- Spirits (Angels, Demons, Djinni, Faeries, Ghosts)
- Shape-shifters (werewolves, etc.)
- Witches, Wizards, and other spellcasters

Magic examples include:

- Abjuration (protection magic)
- Conjuration (banishing/summoning creatures/objects)
- Divination (obtaining knowledge through magical means, including scrying)

- Evocation (summoning and projecting lethal types of energy to destroy objects or enemies)
- Mind Magic (curses, illusion, mind control)
- Nature (elemental energy, communication with plants and animals, healing, weather control)
- Necromancy (destroying or transferring spiritual or physical energy from one person or object to another, speaking to spirits, and raising the dead back to life or as undead)
- Transmutation/Enchantment (changing creatures or objects into another type or adding new abilities to them, either temporarily or permanently, including creating magic items)

Spellcasters may be well-rounded wizards who who know a bit of everything, while others may specialize in mastering a few specific types or subtypes of magic, such as ice witches, shape-shifters, or necromancers.

In some worlds, it may be impossible for casters of one type of magic to use an opposing type, such as fire and ice magic, or nature and necromancy. It may be easier to learn complementary types of magic, such as wind and water magic to help them sail and defeat enemy ships. Perhaps some casters pride themselves on unusual or "forbidden" combinations of magic, such as a necromancer who masters nature magic to heal both the living and undead.

Supernatural heroes can be tricksters or warriors based on their powers and how they use them. Most are introverts who avoid contact with mundanes. With their own kind (or those they trust) they may feel free to act as extroverts.

Examples: Dr. Strange, Gandalf, John Constantine, Damon and Stefan Salvatore from *The Vampire Diaries*.

SUPERNATURAL FLAWS

Perhaps the hero's supernatural powers are only available under certain conditions, or have built-in strengths and weaknesses that limit the hero's effectiveness in specific situations (such as a vampire being strong at night and powerless in daylight), or else her powers are unpredictable (like chaos magic), or come at a high price—for example, reducing her sanity or lifespan with each use, or making her less and less human.

OVERCOMING FLAWS

Since all special heroes wield dangerous, mysterious powers, they should practice to gain mastery of them, and carefully consider the cost to themselves and to others before using them—or Very Bad Things will happen!

ANTI-HEROES

"I'm not sure why I'm so drawn to heroes who do bad things and to villains who think they're the good guys, but I do find that moral ambiguity and conflict makes for great characters."

— BARRY EISLER

IF A CHARACTER DOES UNLIKEABLE THINGS for good reasons, then he's an anti-hero. Humanize him wherever and whenever possible; make us understand why he does what he does the way he that he does it. Make sure the people he is up against are even more ruthless and cruel so your anti-hero looks good by comparison.

A great example of this is Clint Eastwood's "Man with No Name" in *A Fistful of Dollars, For a Few Dollars More*, and *The Good, the Bad, and the Ugly*. Clint's character is a greedy opportunist, but the people he goes up against are even worse.

What makes the "Man with No Name" likable is that he has traits his opponents lack: a sense of humor and moral compass that keep him from ever having to hate himself. There are certain things he won't do, even if it prevents him from reaching his goal. This keeps the "Man with No Name" from becoming a true villain, no matter what crimes he commits. Despite his flaws, he still has a heart, and we love him for it.

We see this type of character time and time again in classic *noir* and crime capers. More recent examples include Johnny Depp's portrayal of "Captain Jack Sparrow" in *Pirates of the Carribbean*, and Billy Bob Thornton's hit man, "Lorne Malvo," in the first season of the *Fargo* TV series.

VILLAINS AND TEMPTERS

"There is a charm about the forbidden that makes it unspeakably desirable."

— MARK TWAIN

WHEN WRITING VILLAINS, the key concept to remember is that the villain believes he is the hero of his own story. He is not there to twirl his mustache and laugh while doing "Very Bad Things" for no discernible reason. That's not a credible villain, that's a cartoon character!

Villains should be the twisted mirror image of your hero. They are what your hero will become should they let their ego control them and surrender to temptation. That's why so many confrontations include some variation of the villain telling the hero, "We are the same, you and I. Only I am not afraid to get what I want."

Rather than just have a hero and villain oppose each other, more complex stories include a third type of character, the Tempter[1]. This character represents what the hero will become should he give in to the villain, and there is usually some backstory involved between the hero and tempter (often a friendly rivalry).

Unlike the villain, the tempter actually respects the hero, and wants to convert him to her side because she genuinely believes he will benefit from it.[2] She may even suggest that if the hero and tempter work together, they can take down the villain far easier than if the hero attempts to go it alone.

The problem is, the tempter often doesn't want to just defeat the villain, she wants to *replace* him. The tempter is guided by a misguided "higher purpose" that justifies her actions. She sincerely thinks she can do a better job than the villain—often in a less villainous way. She will be sincerely hurt when the hero rejects her plan, but will not let it stop her from going through with it.

Perhaps the most famous example is Darth Vader's speech to Luke Skywalker in *The Empire Strikes Back*: "Luke, you can destroy the Emperor. He has foreseen this. *It is your destiny!* Join me, and together we can rule the galaxy as father and son..."

Another great example (from another LucasFilm classic) is the amoral French archaeologist René Belloq, who tries to convince Indiana Jones to help him aid the Nazis for their mutual gain in *Raiders of the Lost Ark*: "All your life has been spent in pursuit of archaeological relics. Inside the Ark are treasures beyond your wildest aspirations. You want to see it opened as well as I. Indiana, we are simply passing through history. This, this *is* history."

The tempter may also exist in a more long-term, harder to resist role as a lover, best friend, or family member. We see this with *femme fatales* in *noir* movies, and corrupt but family-minded business tycoons like J.R. Ewing on *Dallas*.

Like your hero, villains and tempters must believe what they are doing is right, and that their actions are helping someone (even if it's only truly themselves). Unlike heroes, villains and tempters are willing to sacrifice everything to achieve their goals, rarely pulling back from the brink (and being resentful when forced to).

However, it's not enough to simply show your villain or tempter doing bad things. You must show her justifying her actions (either to herself or others), and reveal the emotional toll these nefarious actions are taking on her.

Note that all the hero archetypes and subtypes I describe are available to villains too. Even your supporting cast and minor characters can benefit from them.

~

FOR MORE IDEAS about writing villains, whether human, alien, machine, or monster, be sure to read my bestselling book, *Writing Monsters & Maniacs*. It has everything you need (including plot ideas) to bring your perfect villain to life.

Additionally, if you are writing post-apocalyptic action or survival horror, read my book, *Writing Apocalypse & Survival*. It will walk you through the stages of the apocalypse, zombie virus incubation stages, how law enforcement, prepper, and survivalist characters will act, and much more, including two complete plot templates for on the road or siege scenarios, and how to combine them.

And if you need help describing your villains, I have a full line of *Writers' Phrase Books*, each tackling a different genre.

CHAPTER 6 FOOTNOTES

1 Some writing gurus refer to the Tempter as the Contagonist (*Dramatica*) or Deflector (*My Story Can Beat Up Your Story*). I prefer to use "Tempter."

2 The difference between the tempter and the false mentor and traitor from the next chapter is that the tempter never tries to disguise he's in league with the villain (or even that he is a villain, or at least morally compromised).

The tempter does not rejoice when the hero suffers. Further, the tempter will make at least some sincere, good faith attempt to save the hero from the villain at least once because of the bond they share—but rarely in a way that would permanently mess up the tempter's relationship with the villain. Too much is riding on it.

FALSE MENTORS AND TRAITORS

"I'm a traitor, but I don't consider myself a traitor... There's no special magic [to deceiving people]. Confidence is what does it. Confidence, and a friendly relationship with the [target]. Rapport, where you smile and you make him think that you like him."

— ALDRICH AMES

SOMETIMES A VILLAIN PRESENTS himself to the hero as a false mentor, friend, or ally. Famous examples include Chancellor Palpatine to Anakin Skywalker in the *Star Wars* prequels, Saruman to Gandalf in *The Lord of the Rings*, etc.

The hero remains blind to the warning signs because she loves the villain, or values him for some other important reason. They have something in common that binds them together.[1]

Perhaps the hero thinks she can change the mentor by leading him back on the right path. This creates wonderful opportunities for conflict, and plenty of ways for the reader to get to know the villain far more intimately than they might were he not as present in the hero's daily life.

Despite the hero's best efforts, the villain cannot be changed, and when the hero tries too hard, the villain throws off his disguise and makes his true nature clear. The story then becomes the epic struggle between the hero and her former mentor/ally/friend.

CHAPTER 7 FOOTNOTE

1 Unlike the tempter from Chapter 6, the false mentor and traitor do not act out of love or loyalty to the hero. That does not mean they hate them, just that they only view the hero as a pawn in their scheme.

When their true nature is revealed, the false mentor or traitor will often make a *token effort* to retain the hero's loyalty before fleeing or attacking. However, this is done solely for their convenience, not out of friendship. As such, their words will be lacking sincerity and attempt to motivate the hero through negative appeals to ambition, fear, or greed—rarely to serve the tempter's misguided "higher purpose."

8

REDEEMING THE VILLAIN

"...I definitely need to understand the villains I play. The best cause
pain to anesthetize themselves against their own pain."

— RON PERLMAN

WHEN A GREATER EVIL than the villain himself is present, writers have
another option: What if the villain realizes the true horror of what he
has done? It is in this moment that one of three things can happen:

1. The hero seizes the moment to defeat the villain while he is
   distracted, then takes on the greater evil.
2. The greater evil destroys the villain, either from sensing the
   villain's wavering commitment, or from not caring about
   the villain at all.
3. Or, in the most satisfying version, the villain realizes the
   error of his ways and joins the hero to redeem himself.

Let's go into the third option with more detail. To redeem himself,
the villain must be willing to sacrifice his plans (and usually his life)
for the greater good. That does not mean the redeemed villain should

win the final battle for the hero, merely that they should make it possible for the hero to win. The hero must still do the heavy lifting, or the ending becomes less satisfying. Not as bad as a *deus ex machina*, but still not quite right.

Let's look at *Return of the Jedi* for an example: During the final battle in the Death Star's throne room, Emperor Palpatine unleashes his Sith lightning to torture and kill Luke Skywalker. Darth Vader is overcome by guilt and remorse, and decides he cannot let his son perish anymore than he can continue to serve his diabolical master. Vader kills the Emperor to save Luke, *but that makes Vader the hero* when the original trilogy is supposed to be Luke's story, not Vader's (despite what any revisionist history the prequels might have imposed).

How much more satisfying would it have been were Vader to have sacrificed himself by wounding the Emperor so badly that Luke could have given Palpatine the final blow? It would have made Luke much cooler because then he would not only have saved his father from a life of evil, but killed the most awful tyrant the galaxy had ever seen.

9

SUPPORTING CHARACTERS

"Supporting characters are a great source to use to develop conflict within a story. In their own unique way each one of the supporting characters can create obstacles for the hero to overcome."

— VICTORIA LYNN SCHMIDT, 45 MASTER CHARACTERS

IT'S NEVER BEEN ENOUGH for writers to only develop their hero and villain. To create a truly memorable world that comes alive, nearly every character[1] in the book must have some character development. The amount depends on whether they are supporting cast or minor characters.

For example, Spider-Man has the best supporting cast in comic book history. Who can forget J. Jonah Jameson, Aunt May, Gwen Stacy, or Mary Jane Watson? Even some of his deadliest enemies are his friends when they're not under the influence of their demented alter-egos (Norman Osborn, aka the Green Goblin, or Dr. Curt Connors, aka the Lizard). Talk about conflict!

DEFINING THE SUPPORTING CAST

Your supporting cast includes the hero's love interest, best friend, mentor, and other primary allies—and sometimes rivals. These are the people your hero is willing to sacrifice herself for, and who would gladly sacrifice themselves for her cause. They need to be every bit as likable as your hero, perhaps even more so.

What would *Star Wars: Episode IV* be without Obi-Wan Kenobi, Han Solo, and Princess Leia? Inexperienced farm boy Luke Skywalker isn't interesting enough to carry the picture, let alone save the galaxy.

What about a less vanilla, more badass character like *Hellboy*? Sure, he could take on most enemies by himself, but how much more fun will his adventures be when Abe Sapien, Liz Sherman, and Johann Krauss are along for the ride? (The answer is a lot!)

A ton of other great supporting cast examples exist: Dr. Watson in *Sherlock Holmes*, Tonto in *The Lone Ranger*, etc. The reason these characters exist is to balance the hero, to give him gifts, training, and advice, and to move the story along while deepening it with bonds of love and friendship, romance and rivalry—and some much needed comedy relief and witty banter.

These characters don't even need to be your hero's friends—even disagreeable traveling companions can add a lot of fun. My favorite example is the bandit Tuco[2] (Eli Wallach) in *The Good, the Bad, and the Ugly*. Tuco is loud, stupid, and greedy, almost a cartoon character, yet without his presence, the film becomes too grim. By being such a jackass, Tuco makes both the hero (Clint Eastwood) look more heroic and the villain (Lee van Cleef) more villainous.

Even a lone wolf like James Bond has his Bond girls and supporting characters like Q and Moneypenny. They may not go with him on his adventures, but they put a face on the cause he's fighting for, and are a big part of what he has to look forward to between missions.

FOOTNOTES FOR CHAPTER 10

1 Obviously, you don't need to develop a random waitress who is just a "walk-on" with little to no dialogue or impact on your story, but don't overlook her either! Sometimes, these "walk-ons"can be expanded into making your scenes both more real *and* more memorable. See Chapter 14: Minor Characters for how to do it.

2 Normally, characters who refuse to change must die (literally or metaphorically) at the end of the story, but because Tuco is more jackass than true villain, and because the audience loves him, he gets to live. Whether or not Tuco uses this lucky break to mend his ways or seek revenge is left to the audience's imagination.

OPPOSITES ATTRACT

"Opposites create intense chemistry. There are more chances of fireworks when different people are together than similar personalities."

— SONAM KAPOOR

WHEN DESIGNING SUPPORTING CAST MEMBERS, keep in mind that they should complement each other as well as the hero:

- Being strong where the others are weak, and weak where the others are strong.
- They should be opposites in logic vs. emotion, courage vs. caution, love vs. hate, etc.
- They should have their own back stories, goals, and ambitions. And quirks. Plenty of quirks!
- They should each provide at least one idea that helps the hero and one that hinders him per story. The bigger the help or hindrance, the more readers will like them. That shows they are useful, but not suited to be the star of the show. That's your hero's job.

Perhaps the best example of this is the original *Star Trek* series. You have the brash, charming and ego-driven warrior, Captain Kirk, supported by calm, logical trickster Mr. Spock, and the curmudgeonly and cautious everyman, Dr. McCoy. They're all highly skilled, they all like each and respect each other, but they rarely agree on the best course of action. This makes for constant conflict, from light banter to actual fist fights! And that's what keeps people tuning in to watch them. It's not the genre or the special effects, *it's the characters*. Notice how the three mundane character subtypes are embodied here—you should strive to recreate this dynamic in any ensemble piece.

LOVE INTERESTS

"Immature love says: 'I love you because I need you.' Mature love says: 'I need you because I love you.'"

— ERICH FROMM

WHETHER HEROIC, villainous, or in-between, your hero's love interest should represent the hero's internal conflict—either what he is missing and seeking in his personal life, or his temptation not to change because her way is easier.[1] In this case, the hero must recognize she cannot be good for him in the long run and either decide to end it or succumb to temptation anyway.

By the same token, the hero must represent the same thing to the love interest: the hope for long-term change and wholeness, or the desperate clinging to bad habits in the name of short-term expediency and pleasure.

In stories without a romantic subplot, substitute a supporting character for the love interest and put them in a platonic relationship with your hero such as best friend, business partner, sibling, etc. Everything else remains the same, and this supporting character becomes the most important one in your hero's life, the one he cares about the most (even if he shouldn't).

If the hero fails on his inner journey, he will lose the love interest —often to death (with the hero to blame). However, the hero may also lose her to a rival or to her own ambitions. Due to the hero's bad decisions, she no longer sees him as compatible.

If the hero succeeds on his inner journey, the love interest becomes his personal reward on top of any external ones for accomplishing his outer journey.

IF YOU NEED HELP DESCRIBING romantic situations, grab a copy of my *Romance, Emotion, and Erotica Writers' Phrase Book*. It has thousands of ways to describe love, romance, and intimacy among humans, aliens, and monsters.

CHAPTER 11 FOOTNOTE

1 The *femme fatale* from *noir* is a classic example of this.

THE STAKES CHARACTER

"Being deeply loved by someone gives you strength, while loving someone deeply gives you courage."

— LAO TZU

THE VILLAIN IS HURTING PEOPLE, but you can't show them all or make us care even if you do. Enter the "stakes character." This is a single supporting character (usually a love interest, best friend, or sibling) who your hero loves deeply.

When the villain victimizes this character, the stakes are raised. Before, what the villain did may not have directly affected your hero, but this time, it's personal. Now the hero has no choice but to act. He will not rest until he rescues or avenges the stakes character.

Examples: Mary Jane Watson and Gwen Stacy from *Spider-Man*, Lois Lane and Jimmy Olsen from *Superman*, Uncle Owen and Aunt Beru from *Star Wars*.

Who is your stakes character and how far will the hero go to protect them?

One interesting idea is for the hero to lose the stakes character in stages, rather than all at once (such as from being kidnapped or killed). This will take a different emotional toll on the hero and create additional conflict. Some examples might include:

- The stakes character is jailed or sentenced to prison by the villain
- The stakes character is tempted, seduced, and/or corrupted by the villain
- The stakes character becomes mentally ill and is institutionalized by the villain
- The stakes character becomes physically ill and is hospitalized by the villain
- The stakes character is sent on a dangerous mission by the villain; this can be done knowingly if the stakes character is a soldier, bodyguard, or law enforcement; otherwise, the stakes character is unaware of the danger. In either case, they insist on going, and suffer a series of unfortunate events caused either by the villain or his enemies.

See how that changes things? Of course, these ideas can also be used for the hero as well, particularly if the villain is a false mentor or traitor (as described in chapter 7).

13

DESIGNING THE TEAM

"Once you declare your loyalty to a team, every person who doesn't support that team, it's their job to ruin you, to tell you you're an idiot and to tell you that you made the wrong choice."

— MARK HOPPUS

WHEN CREATING TEAMS OF ALLIES for your hero and villain, they should be mirror images of each other.[1] If the hero has a sidekick, the villain should as well, and that sidekick should complement the villain, just as the hero's sidekick complements him. By complement, I mean they have skills and powers the hero or villain lacks. This creates a more well-rounded team.

And that brings me to a book you absolutely need to read. It's one of my favorites, and it opened my eyes regarding how to create teams. It's called *My Story Can Beat Up Your Story* by Jeffrey Alan Shechter. In it, he states that beyond the hero or villain, there are certain archetypes on every team:

1. a Believer who loves and trusts in the hero and fills the role of sidekick, best friend, and/or love interest;

2. a Protector who embodies the hero or group's moral compass;
3. a Doubter who complains and questions everything;
4. a Feeler who reacts first and thinks later;
5. a Tempter who tries to pull the hero or villain off their path; and
6. a Thinker who analyzes everything before acting.

With smaller casts, some of these roles can played by the same character. In larger casts, you could have more than one of each, but try to make them different—one could be funny, the other serious.

Here are important questions to ask yourself about your teams:

1. Why did the characters join? Most will do so because they believe in the hero or villain's goals, or else supporting the team serves their own agenda (fame, fortune, love, loyalty, revenge, etc.).
2. Remember that only insane bad guys think of themselves as truly "evil" (and even then, only rarely), so give them a strong, logical motive to be on the villain's team. If they are connected to the villain through love, family, or friendship, even better.
3. Give each teammate at least one quirk to make them memorable, and then pay it off, like Indiana Jones being afraid of snakes in *Raiders of the Lost Ark*.
4. Humanize your anti-heroes and bad guys with a few sympathetic traits and/or give them a twisted moral code, such as they refuse to harm innocents.

THE OLD SWITCHEROO

Keep in mind the potential for great drama when one of the hero or villain's team is blackmailed or *willingly* switches sides. Are they double agents, in it for themselves, or had a change of heart?

14

MINOR CHARACTERS

"Minor characters can add spice to your novel, that extra spark that distinguishes the best fiction."

— JAMES SCOTT BELL, REVISION & SELF-EDITING

WE'VE TALKED ABOUT DEFINING the hero and villain's supporting cast. Now, let's take a look at minor characters and how they help flesh out your writer's world.

DEFINING MINOR CHARACTERS

Think about it: Would the scene in *The Empire Strikes Back* where Darth Vader hires Boba Fett have been as good without all the other bounty hunters in the background? Or the creepy bartender ghost Jack Nicholson talks to in *The Shining*? These guys may not get a lot of scenes, but they steal the ones they're in.

Why? Because minor characters ground the hero and villain in the setting. They show us how they interact with those who aren't on their level, but who still possess something they need.

"I always try to keep that in mind—that each minor character who comes on, even if it's only for one scene, has his own agenda, his own ideas, and he's not just there to serve the leads, so to speak."
—*George R. R. Martin*, "On the Craft of Writing"

MINOR CHARACTERS AREN'T ROCKET SCIENCE

They don't need as much development as your supporting cast, so it's often best to assign each minor character a "limp and an eye patch" and move on. By that, I mean a unique trait or two that makes them memorable: a foreign accent, a shifty-eyed look, or a peculiar outfit or hobby. Maybe the character always refers to himself in the third person, like George Remus, that annoying gangster from *Boardwalk Empire*. You get the idea.

HOW MINOR CHARACTERS TURN BORING SCENES GREAT

When your hero or villain enters a potentially boring scene with a minor character, be sure to consider that the minor character wants something too, and recognize the opportunity for conflict this represents.

For example, in Stanley Kubrick's *Eyes Wide Shut*, minor character Mr. Milich (Rade Serbedzija) refuses to let the hero, Dr. William Harford (Tom Cruise), into his costume shop after hours. While Harford grows increasingly desperate, Milich hems and haws, then finally agrees—but only *after* Harford bribes him. Milich then wastes the good doctor's time with weird stories and way too much personal information about his immoral daughter (Leelee Sobieski) and her Japanese "guests" before finally helping the doctor pick out the right costume.

This is a brilliant, hilarious scene and one people remember, even though it has *nothing* to do with the rest of the story. Milich inhabits his own little world. He has no connection to the secret sex club Harford is investigating. Milich exists simply to make a bit of extra trouble for the hero and to provide some much-needed comic relief, but of a kind that fits the disturbing tone of the film.

So the next day, when Dr. Harford returns his costume to the shop, the audience is delighted to see Milich and eager to find out what happened between him and his daughter after Harford left.

Be sure to have one or two scenes like this with minor characters in every story you write. They don't need to be long, they just need to be memorable.

If you are writing a series, find ways to bring the best of these minor characters back. For example, in my urban fantasy novel, *Titan*, I have the heroes summon the fussy ghost of a famous doctor to perform "psychic surgery" on a wounded character. The ghost advances the plot, but he also helps world-build the afterlife of my setting, as well as show off the power of the witch hero who summoned him. The ghost also provides some much-needed comic relief while still being a bit creepy. So naturally, when the heroes travel to the Underworld in the sequels, who they gonna call? No, not *Ghostbusters*! They're going to call the ghost doctor they met in the previous book.

Who knows? If your minor characters prove popular enough, they might merit their own spin-off series or standalone novels. After all, look what happened to Boba Fett: Fans loved him in *The Empire Strikes Back*, hated how he died in *Return of the Jedi*, and so LucasFilm brought him back to life in the *Star Wars* Expanded Universe, as well as for *Attack of the Clones*.

THAT'S IT for characters in general. We'll move on now to discuss the way gender impacts how characters think and feel. Buckle up, it's a bumpy ride...

— JDC

HOW TO WRITE REALISTIC
MEN

INTRODUCTION

Why do so many writers fail to deliver credible, realistic male characters?

Male authors may introduce flat, one-dimensional action-hero types who always kick ass, get the girl, and win the day without ever revealing any true vulnerability. Sure, they may get captured, lose a few allies, and take hundreds of pages to take down the villain, but we don't ever learn anything about the character: his hopes and weaknesses, or what he really fears. These plot-driven books can be fun, but without character growth, the stories become forgettable cartoons.

Female authors may try to create idealized, fantasy versions of masculinity that they are more comfortable with. They don't understand how difficult it is to be a man—not because of our simplicity, but *because* of it. Idealized male characters will appear weak and way too open, both with themselves and with others—especially their love interests. They share their feelings, they aren't afraid to cry, and they don't get mad and storm out of the room or collapse into moody silence when shamed or confronted.

These are the unbelievable male characters that make male readers cringe. Even if the rest of the book is good, a single male character that rings false ruins it. No doubt the same case can be made for female readers who dislike the helpless caricatures many male authors sketch in for their hero's love interests.

In this next quick-start guide, I'm going to demystify male characters by revealing powerful secrets into the psychology of men. These secrets will take your writing to the next level with the complex, credible characters your fiction deserves!

— Jackson Dean Chase
Get a free book at
www.JacksonDeanChase.com

P.S.: This book deals in generalities and is not meant to be a blanket statement about gender. Exceptions to everything can and do exist. By first understanding the basics of how men think and act, it becomes easier to know how and why your male characters are the way they are. You'll also know what happens when your characters deviate from the basics—what they gain, what they lose, and why they think it's worth the trade-off.

WHAT MAKES A MAN A "MAN"

To UNDERSTAND MEN, we first need to understand women. Women operate under many contradictory, complex rules. These rules create a vicious "shame web" that traps women no matter which way they turn, such as:

- "Work hard, but make it look effortless."
- "Dress sexy, but not slutty." (etc.)

Men, on the other hand, have only One Rule:

- "Don't be weak."

This is not the intricate ever-changing web of women, but a *rigid iron box*—a prison that tightly binds our responses. Every decision gets filtered through this One Rule. It doesn't matter if it's stupid, hurtful, or dangerous. And this happens even with the most enlightened, "in-touch with his feelings" kind of guy.

Why? Because he was raised by the One Rule. It's always there, lurking under the surface, no matter how much work he's done to break it. So while a sensitive, confident man may be able to ignore or reject the One Rule, he will always consider it, even if only on a subconscious level.

2

NATURE OR NURTURE

WHERE DID THE ONE RULE COME FROM? Is it nature or nurture? I believe it is both; the desire to compete, to dominate and control our surroundings—and defend our territory—is hardwired in. That desire is then consistently reinforced by other men; those we fear and those we love, both of whom encourage us to be bound by it or pay the cost.

In primitive days, no man wanted to go on a dangerous hunt or to war with a man he considered weak, because that weakness could get his fellow warriors injured or killed. A man had to be strong to contribute to his tribe, let alone attain a position of respect. The minute a leader showed weakness, he was either banished or killed. That's because men don't give up power easily. Few are willing to step down or aside, even to get out of their own way when it is in their best interest or that of their tribe.

What about demotion? Why does a man who loses his power have to be banished or killed? A man stripped of his power tends to harbor deep grudges. He will plot revenge. He will sow disharmony and do anything to make up for the humiliation of his failure.

Male pride demands revenge through the restoration of lost power. That means removing whoever got in his way and toppled him from his position. When revenge and/or restoration are not possible, a man's anger turns inward. He becomes bitter. Defeated. Morose. Petty. Stubborn. He will hate himself for his weakness and find small ways to act out against others, just to relieve the negative feelings that threaten to consume him.

3

WOMEN REINFORCE THE ONE RULE
WITHOUT REALIZING IT

WOMEN SAY THEY WANT A KIND, caring, sensitive man—a man who can be vulnerable. And of course they do, but only to a certain extent. When a man dares to open himself up—to show how truly scared he is—the woman may reject him for not being a "real man."

Again, I believe this is because evolution has hardwired women to seek security for themselves and their offspring. A weak man is a threat to that security. He may not be able to physically protect them, nor be able to provide the resources needed for basic needs such as food and shelter.

A woman wants to take pride in her man, to prove to the rest of her tribe she is clever and attractive enough to catch and keep him. While the genders may express this pride in different ways, a man wants to take pride in his woman every bit as much. To pair with a good mate, a man must be strong and confident.

Sometimes, it seems men can't win. We have to be careful how we share and how much: just enough to be sensitive, but not enough to appear weak. This is a fine line to walk because as soon as a man feels rejected, he learns he can never truly reveal who he is, even to the woman he loves. This is a poison that can kill a relationship.

Men don't want to risk endangering their relationships, so many feel forced to put on an act, a constant strutting, preening show of strength to prevent other men from taking what they consider theirs: jobs, property, possessions, mates, etc.

The irony of course, is that a man who keeps his true self secret from others can ultimately end up losing everything: friends, family, even himself. His life is a charade and all his accomplishments ring hollow.

4

ANGER OR AVOIDANCE

Being confined by the One Rule leaves men two possible responses to shame: anger or emotional withdrawal. Pointing out actual or imagined weakness in a man triggers one of the two, which will eventually trigger the other if the man continues to feel disrespected. Remember, the greater the shame, the stronger the reaction.

Men don't like to feel forced to respond, and when pressured to do so, they may blow up or walk away rather than talk things out. *The One Rule demands it.*

At this stage, a man needs time to heal and get his "head together," sorting through the complex emotions of the situation. He may seek out others to commiserate with, typically other men he feels will offer loyalty and support without fear of judgment.

This healing process can take a few hours to a few days or more. It depends on the severity of the situation, how time-sensitive it is, and how quickly he can come up with solutions.

What are some things men do to blow off steam? Well, it depends on how angry or withdrawn they are. Common attempts at self-medication include the following actions, several of which may be tried or combined before finding the "right" ones:

- Alcohol
- Breaking things
- Cheating
- Criminal acts (speeding, vandalism, etc.)
- Driving, running, or walking aimlessly
- Drugs
- Fighting with people unrelated to the cause
- Sleep
- Sports (either watching or playing)
- Venting to people unrelated to friends
- Venting to family
- Video games
- Watching a movie or TV

Clearly, some actions are more high risk than others. A man prone to relying on one type of action will tend to return to it again and again, using it as a crutch to get him through.

This can be especially problematic if it is illegal or high-risk; if the man is caught or suffers in some way from taking the action, he will often blame the source of trouble that caused him to take the action: boss, coworker, family, friend, etc.

For example, a man in this position might say, "It's your fault I did it! You drove me to it with your bullshit. You just make me so crazy, I don't know what else to do."

Obviously, it's not the other person's fault, it's the man's for making a bad decision when he is not in the right frame of mind. But the One Rule doesn't let the man admit that to himself, not when there are convenient scapegoats nearby. Blaming others is a short-term fix to a long-term problem. It feels good in the moment because it doesn't strip away any more of the man's power at a time when he can least afford to lose it. This is toxic and can destroy a man if he's not careful.

The best thing to do is give a man time to think and heal on his own, then approach him hours later, or even better, wait for him to approach you. It will be hard for him; don't make it harder.

MEN FIX THINGS

WHEN PRESENTED WITH A PROBLEM, men prefer to solve the issue as quickly and easily as possible. We hate to hash over every tiny little detail, but desire to get to the heart of the matter and *fix it*. This minimizes the amount of time we may potentially appear weak. It may not always the best solution, but it is the one we are most comfortable with.

When a woman expresses confidence in our advice and ability to reach a solution, we feel powerful—respected and loved. We are in our element: a strong man fixing things. Any weakness we may have displayed (even if it was only in our own mind) is replaced by feelings of self-worth.

Unfortunately, men and women have different ways dealing with shame. This may cause gender miscommunication, such as in this familiar exchange:

Woman: "I just need you to listen to me!"

Man: "But how will that fix anything?"

But what these two are really saying is:

Woman: "I need to know you love and support me through anything."

Man: "I love you and hate seeing you hurt. It makes me feel weak to do nothing. I want to help by taking tangible, practical action. Let me either fix the problem for you, or help you fix it yourself, but let's do something about it right now."

Now that you understand the psychology of how men process shame and deal with problems, you have the framework not only to write convincing male characters, but to better understand the men in your life.

HOW MEN TALK AND ACT

When not deep in male bonding, men tend to speak and gesture in bold, aggressive ways—these may stem from honest confidence to bluff and bravado.

Our drive to conquer and dominate is fueled by chemistry and culture so much that we find it difficult to stop—even when women react poorly to our words. That's because it's more important to appear strong to ourselves and those around us rather then modify our words and behavior.

Here are some typical male reactions to positive and negative events:

- "I crushed it!"
- "I killed it!"
- "I kicked their ass!"
- "BAM! In your face!"
- "Nailed it!"
- "Ha! You lose, sucker!"
- "You don't get it—they want to destroy me."
- "You want a war, you got a war!"
- "Are you trying to piss me off?"

- "What the hell were you thinking?"
- "They wouldn't dare!"
- "Nobody talks to me that way!"
- "That punk hasn't got the guts."
- "They all think I'm worthless, but I'll show them!"
- "Try that again and you'll be sorry."

You see the bold, violent way we talk? Men speak the language of war, a martial tongue fueled by the desire not just to compete, but control. Because deep down, we're scared if we can't control our environment, we're not strong enough to keep it. Everything is a battle at worst and a game at best. We feel if we could just say or do the right thing, everything else will fall into place and our victory will be assured.

Anything that challenges our position needs to be evaluated for how big a threat it is and how to deal with it quickly and decisively. We express our positions aggressively to not only show others our strength, but to reassure ourselves we can win.

Welcome to the deceptively simple yet unbelievably complicated world of men.

HOW TO WRITE MALE BONDING SCENES

MEN RARELY SIT DOWN with the goal of talking about our emotions. Instead, opening up occurs as a by-product of engaging in another activity such as sports, drinking, etc. The activity makes it safer for us to bring up our problems, as attention can quickly return to the activity if our attempt meets with rejection.

When we feel comfortable, we let our guard down—but only with people we trust. The One Rule is always lurking as we consider how to express our feelings in a way that does not violate the rule. Sometimes words are difficult, and all we can manage are sighs, grunts, or curses. Body language may be used to emphasize mood, such as rubbing our head or chin, putting our face in our hands, or making frustrated gestures. Slumped shoulders are also common.

This is the cue for the listener to begin some vague and gentle questioning to determine what the problem is. The troubled man will use carefully chosen words, often in coded language interspersed with more non-verbal communication (such as long drinks of beer) to allow space to test the listener's response.

Should he not be rejected or ridiculed (at least not too badly), the troubled man may continue to open up. This is when the touching, tender, revealing part of the bonding scene happens, but he will still be cautious, talking *around* his "weakness" until he can come to the heart of the matter. His emotions will cycle between confusion, frustration, fear, and anger.

Now it is the listener's turn to offer advice and encouragement in an attempt at problem-solving. He may offer anecdotes from his own life in an attempt to put the troubled man at ease and provide reassurance he's not the only one to have this problem.

Note that men will use terms such as "bro," "man," or "dude" to express affection in a way that reinforces strength and camaraderie while downplaying weakness. A man rarely says, "I love you," to other men not related to him because that could be perceived as weakness even though it is actually strength.

Most expressions of love among men must pass through the One Rule's filter and come out translated as quick, rough hugs, arm punches, or slaps on the back, often accompanied by "I love you, man," "You're the best, dude," "You got this!" or "You deserve it, bro."

Rarely will a man cry, and when he does, it will usually be when he is sure he is alone. However, if his need is too great, he may cry in front of a best friend, family member, or a trusted father-figure. As a guideline, the only other time male tears are publicly acceptable is for a sports victory, especially a championship.

When a man begins to tear up, he may try to divert attention through an action such as grabbing another beer, looking away, lying or joking that he has "some dust in his eye," going to another room, or leaving the location and not returning until he has his emotions under control.

When a man feels he's reached his emotional limit or the problem has been resolved, he will offer brief, guarded appreciation to the other man for listening. The exchange will end with reassuring "manly" sayings and/or gestures as indicated above. In more formal situations (such as with a mentor about a career problem), a heartfelt handshake may suffice.

This is the signal for both men to ease back into the boundaries of the One Rule by making fun of themselves and/or the problem.

Shared humor reinforces that the men are strong enough to laugh off this danger and have become stronger by talking it out.

Contrast this with the way women relate with each other. With them, weakness is not a concern and affection is easily given, but solutions may take longer to appear, perhaps only after multiple discussions.

HOW TO WRITE REALISTIC
WOMEN

INTRODUCTION

IN THIS THIRD AND FINAL QUICK START GUIDE, I'm going to teach you the top secrets of how to create fully realized, three-dimensional female heroes and villains. I'm going to give you all the same resources, the same research, but I'm going to deliver it in bite-size chunks, with practical examples of the very real and very different challenges women face that men don't. If you're a man (and I assume you are), some of these challenges you may be aware of, others you may not.

Let me shoot the elephant in the room: This is not a boring, politically correct manifesto on feminism or social justice or anything like that. There are plenty of in-depth books on gender equality and women's issues by far more qualified writers. What this book does is provide a unique toolkit for male authors to learn how to write realistic women in the easiest and shortest way possible.

Why should you do this? Beyond the obvious goal of being a better, more well-rounded writer and providing strong role models, there is another incentive—a financial one. Women read more books than men and they also write more reviews. Not just by a little bit, but by a lot! And women naturally want to see themselves reflected in your words. That can't happen if you don't know the secrets contained in this book. These secrets are how you win over female readers, sell more copies, and get better reviews. So don't wimp out.

Are you ready? It's time to man up and write realistic women!

— Jackson Dean Chase
Get a free book at
www.JacksonDeanChase.com

P.S.: Just another reminder this book deals in generalities and is not meant to be a blanket statement about gender. Exceptions to everything can and do exist. By first understanding the basics of how women think and act, it becomes easier to know how and why your female characters are the way they are.

You'll also know what happens when your characters deviate from the basics—what they gain, what they lose, and why they think it's worth the trade-off.

1

GENDER DIFFERENCES IN STORYTELLING

WHEN I WAS RESEARCHING my first novel, I came across Christopher Vogler's *The Writer's Journey: Mythic Structure for Writers*, a book that put the storytelling theory of Professor Joseph Campbell into an easily accessible, digestible formula for writers. It's a great book, but focused solely on the male perspective—which was a problem, since I was writing a novel with a female main character. Then I stumbled across Kim Hudson's *The Virgin's Promise: Writing Stories of Feminine Creative, Spiritual, and Sexual Awakening*. This presented a feminine take on Campbell's theory—again, for writers—and it really opened my eyes to gender differences in storytelling. While men's stories are all about defeating external evil and saving *others*, women's stories are much more about defeating internal evil and saving *themselves*.

In other words, most masculine stories adhere to mythic structure, while most feminine stories adhere to fairy tale structure. That's not to say men can't go on "feminine" journeys (such as Lester Burnham does in *American Beauty*) or women can't go on "masculine" ones (such as Dorothy *The Wizard of Oz*). Part of the fun of being a writer is deciding which kind of journey you want your main character to go on.

MASCULINE AND FEMININE HEROIC JOURNEYS

To differentiate between the two types, *The Virgin's Promise* refers to a female main character going on a feminine journey as a "virgin" (the term in this context isn't sexually-related, but refers to the heroine's unawakened, inexperienced state). The author explains the story difference as:

> The quest of the Virgin is to become all she is capable of being and in so doing create joy and happiness. The quest of the Hero is to assert his will against evil and in so doing overcome fear.
>
> —Kim Hudson, *The Virgin's Promise*

Ms. Hudson goes on to illustrate there are other differences too, most strikingly in the stakes involved:

> The tensions are also different in the Virgin and Hero stories. The cost of the Virgin going on her pathway is the potential loss of love, joy, and passion. Without these things that accompany the fulfillment of her dream, the Virgin suffers loss of self, which manifests as depression, insanity or suicide. The cost to the Hero going on his journey is potentially death. This loss of life at the hands of others will involve physical pain and leave his village vulnerable to evil.

So the Virgin is not likely to die except by her own hand, and neither is her village necessarily doomed (indeed, they may not even understand there is a problem at all). The Hero, on the other hand, has an *extremely* high chance of being killed by his enemies, and everyone in his village understands they will suffer too if he fails. As Kim Hudson explains it:

> Both stories follow an emotional pattern in which the protagonist is at first tenuous, then takes a chance and almost loses, but learns from this experience and finally follows the pathway to success. In short,

they both go through emotional reversals that make for great storytelling."

Until I read *The Writer's Journey* and *The Virgin's Promise*, I was blind to the fundamental gender differences in storytelling. But my journey didn't end there...

2

HOW I LEARNED TO WRITE FEMALE CHARACTERS

WHEN I SET out to write my first novel, I did the math and figured I'd make the main character female. Women buy more books, therefore they must want to read about women. But why would they want to read about ones written by a man? And me specifically?

The problem was, even though I'd been around women my whole life—*had dated them, lived with them, been friends*—I didn't know much about them. Oh sure, I knew they were different than guys, but I had no idea *why*.

If I was going to write an authentic female, it was time to find out!

WHERE TO BEGIN?

I'd always loved *Mean Girls* (underdog stories are my favorite), so I started my research by reading *Queen Bees and Wannabes* by Rosalind Wiseman, the non-fiction book the movie was (loosely) based on. That was revealing, but only whet my appetite for more. A female friend recommended *Reviving Ophelia* by Mary Pipher, and that was helpful too. Brené Brown's *Daring Greatly* further added to my understanding of the complicated, spiraling "shame web" that surrounds women (men, on the other hand, get a prison-type box to hide our shame in).

To quickly summarize, Brown says men live by one rule: "Don't be weak," while women live by an endless supply of contradictory rules: "Dress sexy, but don't look like a slut," etc. And here I thought the one rule men live by was hard—at least it doesn't contradict itself! Since I was writing a dark, edgy book, I also read memoirs like Kerry Cohen's *Loose Girl: A Memoir of Promiscuity* and chick-lit like Martha O'Connor's *The Bitch Posse*. I watched all the hip teen girl shows like *Pretty Little Liars, The Lying Game, Twisted,* etc. Through combining everything I'd learned from all these sources, I quickly and easily learned how female characters acted and reacted to various situations, how they related to others, even to themselves.

Another key book for me was *45 Master Characters* by Victoria Lynn Schmidt, which compared and contrasted the feminine heroic journey vs. the masculine one: the differences in power and support, and how the genders start off in essentially different worlds: Both men and women need to dissolve their ego to awaken. Women *come into* their power to realize their authentic goals and connectedness, whereas men *let go* of their power to realize their authentic goals and connectedness.

> The awakening is like a form of surrender the character goes through, a rebirth into the unknown.
> —Victoria Lynn Schmidt, *45 Master Characters*

This was amazing, fascinating stuff! I was beginning to feel confident I could create complex, believable female characters of any age.

Of course, no book on how to write female characters would be complete without mentioning the Bechdel Test, which is a way to gauge a work's gender bias by asking the following questions:

1. Does the story have at least two women in it,
2. who talk to each other,
3. about something *besides* a man.

A fourth question is often added that asks if these characters are named or not, indicating whether they have any level of importance or not.

Doing this research into writing realistic women not only made me a better writer, it made me a better man, and a better friend to the women in my life.

THE EASY TWO-STEP FORMULA TO WRITING REALISTIC WOMEN

IN *A GAME of Thrones* and its sequels, best selling author George R. R. Martin created some of the most realistic, beloved female characters in fiction. With the notable and annoying exception of Sansa Stark, Martin creates strong female heroes that are a pleasure to read. He does that by making them interesting people who struggle with incredibly complex, dangerous problems—problems that appeal to all readers first and to "women's issues" second.

In fact, most of Martin's "women's issues" aren't boring domestic obligations, pregnancy, or anything like that, but instead they are additional complications to how the character's problems must be solved because they are women operating in a ruthless medieval patriarchy. Because they are women, how they wield power is different than how a man would wield it. The end result may be the same, but how it happens behind the scenes tends to require extra scheming and consensus-building.

If the female character fails to take into account all the fragile male egos involved—and how to juggle them against her own needs—then she is likely to face rebellion, betrayal, or worse far faster than if she were a man.

Because Martin writes his other female characters so well, his

Sansa Stark chapters stick out as exceptionally boring. Sansa starts weak and stays weak. Her chapters are so dull and whiney and involved solely with "women problems," so much that they are unrelatable to male readers. When my friends and I compared notes, we discovered we all skimmed or skipped her chapters, and doing that made no impact on our understanding the story— that means her chapters were essentially worthless. We never dared do that with any of the other female characters—in fact, we looked forward to them.

The writers of the HBO adaptation wisely altered Sansa's character to learn from her unique situation; over the course of the series, she slowly transforms from annoying teenager to calculating political player. If Martin had done that in his books, I guarantee my friends and I wouldn't have skipped Sansa's chapters.

But George R. R. Martin isn't alone in making this mistake. Many male writers think a female character must be obsessed with "women's issues." It's no wonder I cringe whenever my favorite movies or TV shows switch from showing the men involved in danger and fun to show the wives or girlfriends being shrill and boring.

That's because women's problems often revolve around boring domestic issues which cause the characters to come off as burdensome nags that do nothing to advance the plot. Their sole function in the story seems to be to "ground" the male characters in some sense of normalcy to serve as a contrast to their exciting away from home adventures. Either that, or to do something incredibly stupid that gets the men in trouble because the female characters don't understand the stakes or subscribe to some blind, naïve world view.

Think Carmela Soprano, Charmaine Bucco, and the other wives from *The Sopranos* (TV, 1999-2007). Compared to the colorful, exciting male Mafia characters, these women are neither likable nor interesting (at least to men), but they sure take up a lot of screen time. The girlfriends and mistresses get to be a little more fun, but not much. That's because they're bit players designed to titillate viewers with sex while complicating the male characters' already complicated lives.

How many wives and girlfriends—or women in general—from

your favorite movies, TV, books, or comics can you think of who are interesting, dynamic plot movers and shakers? Probably not many, at least not without having to think hard. The only female characters I can remember liking on *The Sopranos* were Tony's suicidal mistress, Gloria, Christopher's nightclub-owning girlfriend, Adriana, and of course, Tony's psychiatrist, Dr. Melfi.

Why? Because these women are the rewards men get, while the wives are the "punishment." But if you take away the men, none of these women would have any impact on the series. They don't have their own stories, not really.

The obvious solution would be to find a way to bring in one or more female criminals, especially one who heads up a rival or allied operation, and one who is just as dastardly as any of Tony's crew. This happens in season two of *The Sopranos*, when Tony goes to Italy and meets a Mafia family run by a woman, and it's beyond wonderful. Unfortunately, her storyline is not continued, and no other female master criminals emerge throughout the rest of the series to take her place.

Of course, no discussion of *The Sopranos* would be complete without mentioning Tony's mom, Livia. This is a strong female character. Her storyline impacts not only the plot, but Tony's entire backstory. She's the reason he has to see Dr. Melfi. Without Livia, there is no special reason why Tony is different from any other mob boss. He'd still be entertaining, but he wouldn't be as nearly as deep and rich a character.

Here's the problem: Livia is a villain. She presents a deliciously real, credible threat to Tony—not just physically (through plotting to have him killed), but mentally and emotionally (through psychologically torturing him his entire life). Livia is definitely a character you'll never forget, and her influence is felt long after she's dead. But villains don't have to be likable, they just have to make viewers love to hate them.

We'll touch on how female villains operate later, but the biggest problem most writers face is getting readers to feel sympathy not just for female heroes, but female *anti-heroes*. Anytime you have women behave outside gender expectations, it's easy to run into trouble. Nowhere is this more prevalent than when writing anti-heroes. A man behaving badly is applauded while a woman behaving the same is not.

House of Cards (TV, 2013-present) attempts to make the male protagonist's wife, Claire, a compelling character and antihero like her husband, but with mixed results. She's mildly interesting as his scheming confidante and ally, but completely cold and unlikable—never more than when her subplot veers into typical boring women's issues, such as when she cheats on her husband, separates from him, and then causes all kinds of annoying, unnecessary political problems. There might have been a way to make that interesting, but the show fails to do that. We'll go into more detail about female anti-heroes later, including what makes them tick and how to make them likable.

Let's get back to talking about heroes. For one of my favorite examples, let's examine *The Rockford Files* (TV, 1974-1980). Hard luck private eye, Jim Rockford (James Garner), is brought a case by well-meaning but shifty lawyer, Beth Davenport (Gretchen Corbett). Beth is an early example of the strong female hero. She's tough-minded and tenacious, putting people before profits which comes into conflict with Jim's mercenary nature. Jim can smell her coming a mile away and groans inwardly every time because he knows what it means... trouble. As a result of her legal crusades, Beth is always getting in over her head and dragging poor Jim along for the ride.

Why do we love her? Beth has an interesting career, charming character flaws, and more importantly, without her bringing Jim all these crazy, horrible cases, there'd be no story. On top of that, she matches Jim word for word in witty banter and constantly outsmarts him by skipping out on what she promised to pay (for noble reasons, though I'm sure Jim would beg to differ). Hell, Beth could have her own series without Jim and I'd watch it. Later on, when the two of them get romantically involved, it's magic. Why? Because the audience has come to love and respect Beth as an interesting person first and as a woman second.

So WHAT DOES ALL this teach us? The trick to writing women that people care about is to follow a simple two-step formula.

STEP 1:
First, make sure your female characters are:
a) interesting people
b) struggling with interesting problems
c) in interesting ways, and

STEP 2:
Make them female.

How do you do that? By making sure your female characters have their own dreams, goals, and desires separate from their romantic relationships with men, and that they have interesting strengths and flaws and quirks and every reason to be in your story.

They cannot exist solely as sidekicks, love interests, or background players. If you want them to be awesome, their actions *must* advance the plot.

Here's another way of looking at it: If you can replace your female character with a lamp for all the good she does, then guess what? *You're not writing realistic women.*

4

HIDDEN PITFALLS OF THE STRONG FEMALE HERO

MANY MALE WRITERS fall into the trap of writing their female heroes like "men with boobs." Don't be one of them. Don't put a strong woman in your story to help it sell, to be "PC," or because you think it's sexy. Just like with any story, the only reason to put a strong female in is if it needs one. She must contribute in meaningful ways that actively move the plot forward. As I've said before, she does this by being an interesting character first and a woman second.

Whatever you do, do not interpret the word "strong" literally. Your female hero doesn't need to be physically equal to men, she just needs to be as smart and as determined, and to have agency of her own.

Even if she's an action hero, she's not necessarily going to be as strong as her toughest male adversaries, though as female body builders have proven, she can certainly come close. It's likely she will compensate with increased cunning and speed, as well as specialized training. She will also be likely to take advantage of the fact that males frequently underestimate female opponents in combat. They hesitate, either from an ingrained societal command not to hurt "the weaker sex" or, if they're bastards, from taking a moment to gloat over the idea of an easy victory. Then, when they realize the fight will be harder than they thought, they get mad. Anger leads to mistakes, which leads to failure. Their shame is not just losing, but losing to a woman.

The strong female's role cannot be to give herself up, to sit around whining and waiting to be rescued, or to lead the male hero to a "higher plane," as in so many love stories and fairy tales like *Cinderella, Rapunzel,* or *Sleeping Beauty.*

She is not the object of the quest, but the one who takes the quest.

Though the quest can (and should) have many components, it must ultimately be about the female's self-realization and self-empowerment. She must shatter whatever male-dominated bonds she had at the beginning and, win or lose, be free to make her own choices at the end.

In a tragedy, she will give up her freedom (and perhaps her life) to help free others even if only by example (such as Joan of Arc).

In a happy ending, she keeps her hard-won freedom and uses it to benefit herself and others. There must be a price to pay and there will be scars (emotional or otherwise), but the woman becomes transformed by her quest. She comes into herself and her power, forcing the people around her to value and respect her on her terms, not theirs.

Beyond the strong female's internal struggle, the way she gears up for her external struggle and assembles her team is different than men. When practical, there will be more planning, talking, listening, and consensus-building, as that's how women tend to get things done. They rarely can bully their way into leadership positions, so they have to be smart about it and consider the feelings of others—or at least pretend to.

The strong female will arm herself sensibly, and select weapons suited to her ability and skill set. And, perhaps most importantly, she will dress sensibly... no chainmail bikinis, no skimpy spandex costumes that show off her body. But why not? Isn't that how women are portrayed when they go into battle? Sure, but have you ever asked yourself *why* they're depicted that way?

Because of the male gaze.

What's that? If you're a woman, you know exactly what it is and how it effects you every day of your life. But if you're a man, you're probably oblivious, so let's break it down.

5

THE MALE GAZE

THE MALE GAZE is the way men in a patriarchal society see and eval-
uate women from the first moment they meet, distorting their
perceived value by how sexually attractive they appear. The less
attractive, the less value, up to the point where the woman ceases to
be seen as her gender at all, but some sort of invisible "it." And an "it"
is tolerated at best, then mocked for her lack of gender and attractive-
ness as soon as her back is turned.

The male gaze sees women first and foremost as objects of pleasure, and secondarily as passive, submissive, and largely irrelevant
"support units" compared to their active, domineering male counterparts. When women attempt to break free from these male miscon-
ceptions, they are met with resentment ("what a bitch!"),
condescension (aka mansplaining), or increased sexual attention.

Whether that male attention is an honest expression of heightened
interest and attraction or used as a weapon to put the woman in "her
place," the problem is that men are viewing her through the male gaze
and not evaluating her ideas or other contributions objectively.

The male gaze pollutes pop culture and all aspects of the media by
trivializing women, infantilizing them, and holding them up to
impossible ideals—not just of beauty, but of who women can be at

home, in the workplace, in relationships—basically in all aspects of their lives.

There is a true power disparity here, and is it any wonder that this patriarchal enforcement of gender stereotypes breeds so much unhappiness and confusion? Is it really so mysterious that women still suffer the burden of navigating our male-dominated society? Of being paid less, charged more, then hitting the glass ceiling and told sorry, that's as far as you get?

Imagine how you would feel if a bunch of oppressive, aggressive men told you what you could do with your body and what your rights were? These men use everything they have to keep you down, from religion to politics to business to culture, all in the name of "protecting" you when they are really only protecting themselves. They use media to control you, to brainwash you into conforming to what they think you should look like and how you must behave.

Imagine how crazy-making it would be to receive a constant stream of conflicting advice: "look sexy, but not too sexy," or "work hard, but make it look effortless." And not just to hear this from men, but other women as well!

That's because some women, not seeing any other choice, "go along to get along." They resent it when they see other women break that mold and will attempt to stop them. It's the old analogy of "crabs in a barrel"—when the captured crabs spot one of their own climbing out of the barrel, they pull her back down to suffer alongside them.

As if that wasn't bad enough, now consider how women's personal safety and right to go about their day unmolested is constantly challenged by men, from catcalls of "Hey, baby!" to serious attempts to seduce you wherever you go. A woman sitting alone in a bar is seen as in need of a man, while a man in a bar simply needs a drink.

And then there's the danger of being assaulted or raped. That is why women think twice about walking down dark alleys or through deserted parking lots. It's also one of the reasons they travel in groups —not just for the social aspects, but so they can look out for each other.

When women do get into relationships with men, they may run

into him resenting her if she makes more money or tries to take too much control. Then there's the risk of the man only wanting her for sex, and the risk of her getting pregnant. Even if things go well, over time, as the woman ages and her attention shifts from him to their children or other responsibilities, the man's eyes might wander to a younger, sexier woman. Women are never safe from the male gaze—whether it is directed at them or others.

When many male writers try to create active, strong female heroes, their vision is still clouded by the male gaze. They simply superimpose "strong" male personality traits over sexually idealized female bodies. The results are cartoon characters whose "strength" is judged by how many men they can seduce, manipulate, or physically defeat in traditionally masculine ways.

So how do male writers create strong female characters? The obvious way is to make her not so much about her appearance, but who she is on the inside. This is the plucky plain Jane who succeeds in a male-dominated world despite her "failure" to arouse the male gaze, at least in a conventional sense.

Think Peggy Olson (Elisabeth Moss) from *Mad Men* (TV, 2007-2015). Over the course of the series, Peggy rises up from lowly secretary to advertising executive. And she has to do it the hard way, by proving the strength of her ideas all while constantly being put down, resented, or ignored by her male counterparts. Because the male gaze devalues Peggy, every day for her is a struggle. And when she screws up (even if it isn't really her fault), she can't fall back on her sexuality to save her. She's likely to be demoted, fired, or humiliated with impunity by the men around and above her.

Because of her gender, Peggy has to work twice as hard to get the same rewards and even then, usually has to settle for less pay, less prestige. She is seen as an anomaly because of her sex and her ambition to compete in a traditionally male job. She may even be pitied by other women because she is busy working instead of finding a husband and raising children.

Do you ever wonder why so female characters in books written by women are described as plain or otherwise atypically appealing to men? Because when a male character falls for her, and/or when he learns to respect and value her, it's not for what she looks like: *It's for who she is.*

Should all your female characters be plain or homely? Of course not! A less obvious and more challenging way to write a strong female is to make it *more* about her appearance, not less. But the trick here is the story is about her having to deal with the constant annoyance of the male gaze and how what she is seen as and lusted after by them conflicts with who she is on the inside.

Mad Men provides another perfect example in Joan Harris (Christina Hendricks), who rises up from being head of the secretarial pool and the mistress of one the ad agency's founders to being a partner in the agency. She has plenty of brains, talent, and ambition under all that sexuality, and uses everything she has to get what she wants. But given the choice, Joan prefers to use her brains more than her body. Even though she appreciates her sexuality's usefulness, she hates herself for having to rely on it to get ahead. But because men enjoy looking at her, Joan would have to do something pretty stupid to ever be demoted, fired, or otherwise humiliated.

Because the male gaze values her, Joan's life is easier than Peggy's in some ways and harder in others. She has to fight to be heard because "any woman that pretty can't be smart," and then when she is finally heard, she has to struggle with the result of that success, which is the man she is influencing wanting to sleep with her—even feeling like "she owes it to him" for helping her! And if Joan does not return that affection, the man may lash out and renege on his promises.

Using seduction and manipulation becomes part of Joan's strategy —not because she'd be a fool not to use it—but because men simply give her no choice. She has something they want, and as long as they stay interested and she can keep that sexual tension going, those men are far more likely to do what she says. The risk with this strategy is when one or more of the men insist on her giving them what they want. Even if she rejects him and gets what she wants, others will still accuse her of sleeping her way to the top because "that's the only way a woman who looks like her can get what she wants."

Because of her beauty, Joan's short-term challenges are easier to overcome than Peggy's, but Peggy has the long-term career advantage: Because the men she is dealing with most likely do not want to sleep with her, they have to at least grudgingly come to value and respect her as a person. Maybe not as much as a man, but close enough where she can get more or less get what she wants eventually, though she will always have to keep fighting... if not the old guard, then all the men coming up under her who have not learned to respect her yet.

As Joan ages and her beauty fades, her ability to influence men diminishes because the male gaze values youth as well as as beauty. Because she relied on her sexuality to get ahead, her ability to get what she wants through who she is instead of what she is will not be as advanced as Peggy's. This ticking clock says women get less sexy as they age and its the primary reason Joan pushes so hard to get what she wants as fast as possible. Since the clock has far less effect on Peggy, she can afford to take the long view more than Joan.

Makes sense? Great! But maybe you don't write workplace dramas like *Mad Men*. Maybe you write science fiction or fantasy. Everything I teach in this book applies as long as your world roughly conforms to our own past or present. Things only change if your society moves from a patriarchy to a gynarchy or a gender-neutral society based on individual merit.

6

"THERE CAN BE ONLY ONE!"

FORGET WHAT *HIGHLANDER* TAUGHT YOU. One of the biggest problems male writers run into is only including a single strong female character. Why is that a problem? Because then she becomes a token, an anomaly. You can point to her and say, "See? I'm a feminist! I put a strong female hero in my story." Um, no. You need to put more than one strong female character in your story to pass the Bechdel Test.

The second female doesn't have to be the same kind of hero as the first, and it's often better if she isn't. For example (again), Peggy Olson and Joan Harris in *Mad Men*.

In a fantasy, you could make one woman a barbarian warrior, the other a thief and wizard, like a female version of Fritz Lieber's legendary Fafhrd and the Gray Mouser.

In a science fiction story, make one woman a tough space marine and the other a cunning warrant officer. Think Jenette Vasquez and Ellen Ripley in *Aliens* (1986)—they're both strong, but they're very different characters.

But if you want them to be the same, you can. Think Robert E. Howard's Conan the Barbarian and Red Sonja or Xena and Gabrielle from *Xena: Warrior Princess* (TV, 1995-2001). They're all warriors, but they were raised differently, trained differently, and have different fighting styles. Regardless of what makes them different, what keeps them together?

Bonus points if you include three or more strong female characters in your story. Three? Maybe that seems like a lot, but it really isn't. Again, you should find a way to differentiate your characters both personally and professionally.

Think Captain Kirk, Mr. Spock, and Dr. McCoy from *Star Trek* (TV, 1966-69). Kirk's bold, Spock's logical, and McCoy's a skeptic. They complement each other and it is the combination of their skills and personalities that allows them to survive. Plus, the endless bickering, jokes, insults, and rivalries are hilarious.

Now that you've got the concept, there's no reason you can't do that with female characters. Think *Buffy the Vampire Slayer* (TV, 1997-2003), *Charmed* (TV, 1998-2006), *The Vampire Diaries* (TV, 2009-2017), or *Pretty Little Liars* (TV, 2010-present). Each of these shows found a successful way to incorporate multiple strong female heroes.

THE PROBLEM OF THE MARY SUE
AND MANIC PIXIE DREAM GIRL

IT WOULD BE remiss of me not to mention—and to caution you against using—two of the most common (and hated) tropes writers resort to when creating female characters:

1. the "Mary Sue" and
2. the "Manic Pixie Dream Girl"

Many women hate these tropes because they are gimmicks, not reality. But not all women hate them, of course, and not all men. Of the two, women prefer the Mary Sue, while men prefer the Manic Pixie Dream Girl. I believe that is because each offers a specific type of wish fulfillment:

- What woman does not want to be perfect and find her perfect love?
- What man does not want to fall in love with a fun, adventurous woman that helps him become a better man?

The Mary Sue has no meaningful flaws. She may start in a lowly position, but she is already "perfect" as a woman and a hero. The reason Mary Sues don't work is they have no depth.

While there is a certain amount of controversy and debate around who is (or isn't) a Mary Sue, some of the best known examples being discussed on the internet are:

- Cinderella from *Cinderella* (1950)
- Princess Aurora from *Sleeping Beauty* (1959)
- Lara Croft in *Tomb Raider* (2001)
- Bella Swan in *Twilight* (2009)
- Elena Gilbert from *The Vampire Diaries* (TV, 2009-2017)
- Katniss Everdeen from *The Hunger Games* (2012)
- Beatrice "Tris" Prior from *Divergent* (2014)
- Imperator Furiosa from *Mad Max: Fury Road* (2015)
- Rey from *Star Wars: The Force Awakens* (2015)

As you can see from this list, Mary Sues are pure of heart and good at everything they do. They are the "chosen ones," destined by birth or circumstance for some epic love or grand adventure that will change the world, but why? It's certainly not their personality! Mary Sues may be pretty, they may be talented, but there's no special reason to like or follow them, and certainly not to love them.

Isn't charisma important? Charm? Personal magnetism? Mary Sues exhibit few to none of these qualities. They are stand-ins for the author and reader, offering wish-fulfillment, nothing more.

Want to find out if your character is a Mary Sue? Take the Bechdel Test free online (Google is your friend).

THE MANIC PIXIE Dream Girl is a free spirit, a love interest who comes into the male hero's life and turns it upside down with her girlish charm and ridiculous quirkiness. By forcing him out of the rut his life is in, she leads him to a higher plane but often disappears or dies at the end. And no one cares. The Manic Pixie Dream Girl doesn't work because she is only in the story to help the male character change. She's a plot device, not a real character.

Some of the wackiest and best known examples of the Manic Pixie Dream Girl are:

- Susan Vance from *Bringing Up Baby* (1938)
- Sugar "Kane" Kowalczyk from *Some Like It Hot* (1959)
- Holly Golightly from *Breakfast at Tiffany's* (1961)
- Annie Hall from *Annie Hall* (1977)
- Vivianne from *Pretty Woman* (1990)
- Belle from *Beauty and the Beast* (1991)
- Mary from *There's Something About Mary* (1998)
- Penny Lane from *Almost Famous* (2000)
- Polly Prince from *Along Came Polly* (2004)

While the characters in these examples may be fun and exciting in a temporary sense, they are ethereal bits of nothing, childish fluff that's impossible to cling to.

Manic Pixie Dream Girls don't live in the real world, but rather one of their own invention that has a completely different set of rules. Maybe that's why they won't (or can't) stick around, and we're better off when they're gone.

Honestly, these characters remind me more of *The Cat in the Hat* by Dr. Seuss than anything else, and like the Cat, they can be just as troublesome, even dangerous when you apply their wacky schemes to reality.

Looking for ways to know if your character is a Manic Pixie Dream Girl?

ANOTHER WAY TO tell if you've written a Mary Sue or Manic Pixie Dream Girl is to see if they have a character arc. If your character doe not grow and change in a dramatic and meaningful way, she may be a Mary Sue or Manic Pixie Dream Girl. Then again, she may simply be a catalyst hero, one who comes into the story already fully formed. A catalyst's mission is to force the other characters to arc. Catalysts are more common to series than standalones.

Note that by "fully formed" I don't mean flawless. For example, James Bond has several deep character flaws he seldom bothers to examine, much less rein in. He glories in them instead (misogyny, narcissism, and racism). Dirty Harry is another series character written in a similar vein. It is these flaws that make them interesting and prevent them from being the male equivalent of Mary Sues.

So why aren't more female series characters expressing similar flaws? Why are they stuck being perfect and perfectly boring? Is it because people are more willing to accept—even embrace—negative qualities in a man, but not in a woman? Is there a double standard, and if so, can it be broken?

8

FEMALE ANTI-HEROES: A SLOW
SLIDE INTO HELL

A RECENT THEORY suggests there may be key differences in the way men and women hate (and forgive). If true, these play a critical difference in how your characters react. According to the theory:

- Men tend to hate groups for life, but find it easier to forgive individuals.
- Women tend to hate individuals for life, but find it easier to forgive groups.

The reason for this may be hardwiring from our primitive past, a past where men relied more on certain key individuals for survival where women relied on groups. Because men have traditionally had more agency and freedom to act, they feel empowered to continue taking revenge far beyond the individual level. Whereas women have not had the same agency, and therefore tend to limit themselves to "safe," small-scale revenge. You can see this difference played out in to this day in modern revenge stories.

In the *Death Wish* series (1974-1994), architect Paul Kersey (Charles Bronson) takes a stand against criminals. Once he serves up vigilante justice to the scum who raped and murdered his wife and daughter, he doesn't stop there. He keeps hunting criminals completely unrelated to his personal revenge. He can't stop because he has nothing left to live for; killing becomes his identity.

In the *Dirty Harry* series (1971-1988), cop Harry Callahan (Clint Eastwood) has a similar problem with crime; crime briefly personified by the villain(s) of each film, but his war is never over. There's always more crime to fight. And both Kersey and Callahan have another group to hate: the justice system, for its failure to help the innocent and for letting violent criminals go on technicalities.

Compare that to Beatrix Kiddo (Uma Thurman) in *Kill Bill* (2003), who is only interested in avenging herself on the specific individuals who wronged her. She kills others, sure, but just to get to the names on her list. Or Jennifer (Camille Keaton) in *I Spit On Your Grave* (1978), who is content to stop being a vigilante after she avenges herself on her rapists.

Exceptions of women hating groups certainly exist, like Thana (Zoe Tamerlis) in *Ms. .45* (1981), who becomes a deranged vigilante killer, or Carrie White (Sissy Spacek) in *Carrie* (1976), who seeks a wider revenge beyond just her immediate bullies, murdering the entire school who humiliated her.

The differences in how the genders hate and forgive may also play a role in how female anti-heroes are received. People expect to be entertained by men acting out of control, but when they see a woman do it? Not so much. That's where gender bias comes in.

Audiences love to watch male anti-heroes like Tony Soprano (*The Sopranos*), Don Draper (*Mad Men*), and Walter White (*Breaking Bad*, (TV, 2008-2013) do all kinds of shitty things. They expect it, they want it, they demand it! And it does little to change the character's likability. But when a female character does something similar, she's often hated. Whatever respect or affection audiences may have had for her goes right out the window. (Case in point: Skyler White on *Breaking Bad*.)

Because women are supposed to be likable, she's instantly and forever hated. Especially by men. They see her as a traitor, a nag, a bitch, a dummy, a whore, even a lunatic! But most importantly, they see her as a *killjoy*. Her only purpose in the story is rewired in the male mind as to stop men from having fun. And while female audiences will likely take the opposite view, that doesn't mean they always will if the character's actions violate too many of the "rules" of being a woman. In short, it's complicated.

I love to write dark, complex female anti-heroes with villainous tendencies. The way I succeed is by not starting off in that dark place. I slowly introduce her to the reader in likable ways. Likable, but flawed. As she continues to pursue her goals, she feels forced to take increasingly drastic actions. The more drastic the action, the more delusional my anti-hero becomes trying to justify what she's doing is the right thing, the only thing. Eventually, she snaps, and that's when the real fun begins...

This strategy only works because I took the time to set it up. It's a slow slide into hell, never a sudden about-face. That's how you win audiences over to your female anti-hero: warming them up.

For strong female anti-heroes audiences of both genders love, I recommend watching Veronica Sawyer from *Heathers* (1988), Gemma Teller-Morrow from *Sons of Anarchy* (TV, 2008-2014), and Norma Bates from *Bates Motel* (TV 2013-2017).

For more thoughts on this subject, read the Huffington Post article, Anatomy of the Female Anti-Hero by Lauren Duca.

9

WOMEN IN PRISON

WOMEN HANDLE PRISON differently than men, and often far better. If your story involves women behind bars, such as *Orange Is the New Black* (TV, 2013-present), *Chained Heat* (1983), or *Prisoner: Cell Block H* (TV, 1979-1986), you'd do well to read *In the Mix: Struggle and Survival in a Women's Prison* by Barbara Owen:

> ...Like most experiences, imprisonment and its subsequent response is a gendered one. ...[Female prison] culture develops in ways markedly different from the degradation, violence, and predatory structure of male prison life.
> —Barbara Owen, *In the Mix*

In the Mix covers everything you need to know about how prison conflict is resolved and relationships built, as well as the home and street life that sends women to prison, the difference between "inmates" and "convicts," how to gain and give respect, relationships with corrections officers, etc. For example, in one of Ms. Owen's many interviews, a prisoner revealed:

"If an officer raises his or her voice to you, some women are petrified. The fear from past abuse comes back and they are scared."

Most of the conflict in women's prison is verbal. The primary danger is not from violence, but manipulation. As one officer who worked in both male and female prisons put it:

"[Male prisoners] will try to game you but will give up. Women will continue over a much longer time; they are more patient, will work on you a little bit at a time... there is also the problem of sexual manipulation here. Females have natural resistance to seduction— males do not and it can get you in trouble..."

So it's not surprising that seventy percent of female prisoners prefer dealing with male staff. As one prisoner explained:

"We have learned to get around men with tears or flattery. None of that works on the female staff because they know it is bullshit."

FEMALE VILLAINS: PUTTING
LIPSTICK ON THE DEVIL

LIKE HEROES AND ANTI-HEROES, strong female villains should also find a home in your stories, but not as stereotypes. The success of any story relies on the strength of its villain.

Make sure your villains are interesting people struggling to solve interesting problems in interesting ways. Two great examples from classic films are Brigid O'Shaughnessy from *The Maltese Falcon* (1941) and Norma Desmond from *Sunset Boulevard* (1950). Both different, both dangerous! One sane, one insane. One young, one old. Both try to creatively problem solve in very female ways as opposed to the male villains in their films.

Villains come in two types: loners and those who either hide behind or act under the authority of a group. Female villains who wish to enact large-scale evil use groups, while those interested in smaller, more personal evil tend to go it alone.

Looking at this further, it seems likely that female villains acting in groups are charming and functional enough to be sociopaths, while those operating alone trend toward psychopaths—unless they are possessed of so much personal power they do not require the support of a group to enact their large-scale plans. Maleficent, the sorceress from *Sleeping Beauty* (1959) is one such example, and Jean Grey/Dark

Phoenix from *The Uncanny X-Men* comic book (issues #101-108, 1976-77 and #129-#138, 1980) is another.

FEMALE VILLAINS WHO USE GROUPS

- The Wicked Witch from *The Wizard of Oz* (1939) uses an army of men and flying monkeys
- Elizabeth Bathory from *Countess Dracula* (1971) uses her aristocratic position and estate
- Nurse Ratched from *One Flew Over the Cuckoo's Nest* (1975) uses her position of authority in a mental hospital
- Katherine Wentworth from *Dallas* (TV, 1978-1991) uses an oil company
- Alexis Carrington from *Dynasty* (TV, 1981-1989) also uses an oil company
- Angela Channing from *Falcon Crest* (TV, 1981-1990) uses a winery
- Diana from *V* (TV, 1984-85) uses an alien invasion force
- Nancy Downs from *The Craft* (1996) uses a coven of witches
- Regina George from *Mean Girls* (2004) uses a clique of rich girls
- Nina Myers from *24* (TV, 2001-2010) uses a federal counterterrorism agency
- Cersei Baratheon from *Game of Thrones* (TV, 2011-2018) uses an entire kingdom
- Mariah Dillard from *Luke Cage* (TV, 2016-present) uses her criminal and political connections

FEMALE VILLAINS WHO ACT ALONE

- Maleficent from *Sleeping Beauty* (1959)
- Carmilla Karnstein from *The Vampire Lovers* (1970)
- Evelyn from *Play Misty for Me* (1971)

- Margaret White from *Carrie* (1976)
- Pamela Voorhees from *Friday the 13th* (1980)
- Alex Forrest from *Fatal Attraction* (1987)
- Annie Wilkes from *Misery* (1990)
- Catherine Tramell from *Basic Instinct* (1992)
- Hedra Carlson from *Single White Female* (1992)
- Asami from *Audition* (1999)
- Samara from *The Ring* (2002)
- Esther from *Orphan* (2009)

HAIR, FASHION, MAKEUP: WOMEN'S CHAINS, WOMEN'S ARMOR

I SAVED this chapter for last because while it's important, it's the *least important* thing you need to know about writing realistic women. Just like the women in your life, what matters most is what's *inside* your female characters. Who they are, what they want. The rest is just window dressing.

Now that I've put this chapter in perspective, let's get started!

HAIR, fashion, makeup... We all know many women are obsessed with getting them "right," at least to some degree. Unlike men, who can just roll out of bed, throw on whatever's handy, and call it good, women can't. Well, they can, but they will be judged for it.

Harshly.

To avoid that judgment, many women will spend at least an hour or two getting ready to leave the house, and more time later if they intend to go somewhere special, like on a date or to a party. That adds up to a lot of hours staring into closets and mirrors.

Then, when they finally do go out, there's a ton of comparing themselves to other women going on. Women notice details men don't, from the exact shade of lipstick to the style of outfit to the brand of shoes. Men could care less, seeing only the broad strokes if they notice them at all.

The makeover is something every woman does sooner or later, often as a response to some setback or rejection. It can be subtle, but is often dramatic. The worse the situation, the more drastic the change. While your story may not call for such a scene, it will almost certainly call for some scene involving hair, fashion, and makeup.

As men writing about women, it's pretty much impossible for us to get all that stuff right. Even if we do a ton of research, we'll still get it wrong. Maybe not all of it, but enough to look stupid to female readers. So how do we solve that?

By avoiding it as much as possible.

My advice is not to sweat the details. It's too easy to get bogged down. Provide the bare minimum information and move on; you can get female friends, editors, or beta readers to fill in specific details later.

Here are some examples of hair, fashion, and makeup scenes from my upcoming vampire novel, *Forever Dark*. Each example provides just a few key details (vetted for accuracy by my female editor and beta readers).

Later that night, Naomi and I snuck a bottle of vodka from her mom's liquor cabinet to celebrate. We mixed it with fruit punch, got buzzed, then spent a couple hours playing with my hair and makeup. After all, if I looked good enough on the outside, maybe Scott would notice I wasn't so bad on the inside.

"That's it," Naomi said. "I think we've got it."

I studied myself in the mirror, turning this way and that in the black stretch minidress Naomi had bought for me. Was it enough?

"Relax," Naomi said. "Scott will take one look and instantly fall in love. He'll say, 'Oh my, you're too beautiful for words'! and just be all..." She exaggerated falling over backwards with one hand draped across her forehead, fake-fainting like in one of those old movies. She fluttered her eyelashes and sighed dramatically.

We both had a good laugh. And another drink.

"My turn," Naomi said. "I need some practice looking hot too."

We did her mahogany curls in an updo and set off her light brown eyes with some olive green eyeshadow. Her eyes really popped, the gold flecks standing out like glitter.

"You look totally sexified."

Naomi beamed, admiring herself in the mirror.

Note that I don't go on and on about every little thing; I focus on how the hair, fashion, and makeup make my characters *feel*. And feeling good is the whole reason women are so into all this stuff in the first place. It gives them a sense of power and control. They see it as armor, their first line of defense against a world that's stacked against them.

The next morning, Naomi's dad picked her up at noon. I was at the mall twenty minutes later, my Hello Kitty backpack full of everything I'd need for my date. I wandered around till I got bored. M·A·C gave free makeovers, so that seemed like a good way to kill time. When I got there, a heavily made-up brunette stood behind the counter.

"Hi," I said, "I'm going out with this new guy tonight, and I want to look really hot."

"No problem." The girl came around the counter and sat me in the makeover chair. "First, we have to get this old makeup off." She wiped a cleansing pad over my face, then applied base with a sponge and brushed on loose powder. "I'm going to add some primer to your lids to make the shadow really dark." She smudged charcoal-gray around my eyes, then pale silver highlighter on my brow bones. Liquid eyeliner and two coats of mascara followed. A matte lip finish completed the makeover.

"Well?" she asked. "What do you think? It's a whole new you, right?"

"Yeah, but I can't believe it! I never thought I could look this good." The M·A·C girl had erased my face and replaced it with something out of my dreams. It was ravishing. Unreal. A stranger's face, yet it was mine.

While that scene goes into a lot more detail, the rough draft went something like this: "Cindy goes to the mall to get a makeover. She now feels empowered to overcome her fear of disappointing Scott. Fill in details later." If I had tried to get that makeover scene perfect in my rough draft, it would have been a joke and my novel would never be finished. So I outsourced the details to my editor, then prettied it up later. The result is a realistic makeover scene written in my own voice.

Since I already have one fairly explicit makeover routine, when the time came for a second, I didn't waste time going into details again, just cut right to the end result:

I did my hair in an updo fastened with rhinestone clips, then swung by M·A·C to get another free makeover. When it was done, I looked like a model. Between the makeup, the dress, and my powers, how could Scott resist?

That's a lot easier to write and still gets the point across. The reader already has the details from the previous makeover, so there's no point going into them again.

Here's an example of a bare bones hair and makeup routine. Again, note how I focus on how the ritual makes her *feel*. What she actually looks like is less important.

I got ready for school, putting a lot of effort into my hair and makeup. When it was done, I looked amazing. Radiant. Glowing.

Up until now, the examples have dealt with looking good. Now let's take some time to explore what women go through when they're not looking their best:

I pulled down the vanity mirror and cringed at my tangled hair and bloody mouth, the darkly staring, hollow eyes. I wiped my mouth and chin with Kleenex from my purse, then aimed the heat vents at my hair, using my fingers to comb through the worst of the tangles. Once it was dry enough, I pointed the vents at my dress while I fixed my makeup. I popped a pair of mints, ignoring the oddly bitter flavor.

Eventually, the girl in the mirror resembled me. Enough to pass for human.

When a female character is not paying attention to her appearance, it may signify something is terribly wrong, as in the following example:

When I got to Naomi's, she answered the door wearing baggy sweats and no makeup.

"Sorry I took so long," I said. "I had to do some stuff for my mom."

"What the hell? You could have texted."

I apologized again as we went into the kitchen. She offered me a Diet Coke. I chugged it, hating the taste but needing the caffeine, then opened another.

Naomi watched me irritably. "Thirsty much? Come on, let's go to my room. My mom'll be home any minute, and we need to talk."

Note that Cindy (the POV character) does not acknowledge Naomi's disheveled appearance, but immediately recognizes her friend is in trouble. She immediately switches to apology mode, not wanting to upset her friend further, then waits for Naomi to tell her what's going on.

If this were a scene with two male characters, the first thing the POV guy might say would be like, "Dude! You look terrible," possibly followed by an affectionate insult or simple, "What's up?" But that's only if his buddy wasn't normally a slob, and if he even bothered to notice something was wrong in the first place.

Why the big difference? Because men favor blunt, direct communication, while women tend toward subtle, indirect communication (unless they're really angry). That's an important detail to understand if you want to get your female dialogue right.

LESSONS I'VE LEARNED WRITING CROSS-GENDER CHARACTERS

CROSS-GENDER WRITING DOESN'T HAVE to be hard—if you do your research. It also helps to get Beta readers, a close friend, and/or an editor of the opposite sex. That's what I did with my Young Adult novels and short stories, and it absolutely made me a better writer, and a better man.

In her reviews of my YA books, Melanie Marsh at Fang Freakin' Tastic Reviews says: "[Jackson Dean Chase] perfectly captures the feelings of being that awkward teen girl. I know because I was that girl," and "Jackson has a way with words that leaves me in awe of his understanding of the female psyche." These quotes were incredibly validating for me as a male author who (so far) exclusively writes female main characters and almost always in the first person.

I'm not saying I have a perfect understanding of the female psyche because as a man, that just isn't possible, just like it isn't possible for a woman to have a complete understanding of what it's like to be a man. *But it is possible to get close*—if you're willing to do the work and immerse yourself in how men think. Consume their fiction, their movies and TV. See not only what they respond to, but *how* they respond. Men and women are different genders, not different species. You'll be surprised how much is the same.

I can't recall who first said it, but I like to keep this quote in mind: "Men and women want pretty much the same things—women just like to talk about them more."

ROLE-PLAYING GAMES

Another trick—and one I recommend highly—is to play characters of the opposite sex in pen and paper role-playing games (RPGs) like *Dungeons & Dragons, Star Wars, Call of Cthulhu*, etc.

You should be looking to join a group that plays a game in the same or similar genre(s) you write in. Multiple RPGs exist for just about any genre or subgenre you can think of: fantasy, horror, hard-boiled/noir, sci-fi, secret agents, steampunk, superheroes, etc. The problem isn't finding a game, it's picking one!

With the right group, you can quickly and easily immerse yourself in what it's like to not be you *or* your gender. It's like acting, but interactive storytelling you make up as you go along. You and the other players each take on the role of a single character within the world, while the Game Master takes on the role of everyone else (the NPCs, or "non-player characters").

Particularly shocking for me within the game world were the constant unwelcome advances and insults my female character endured from male NPCs, along with the frequent inability to be heard, respected, or understood by them. I was viewed as a "support unit" rather than a hero, and had to work twice as hard to be recognized as one. It was extremely challenging, but ultimately rewarding.

Aside from immersing myself in female pop culture and psychology, I credit role-playing with giving me the biggest leg up when it came time to write female-driven fiction.

You can often find gaming groups recruiting new players at your local comic book shop. Ask the owner or check the bulletin board. It may help to explain you're an author trying to achieve better cross-gender writing by experiencing what it's like to be a male hero. Who knows? You may get some extra beta readers—and fans—from the group!

AFTERWORD

I'm profoundly grateful to the writers who made this book possible, and to all the women—*especially my editor*—who shared their amazing advice and stories while helping me whip this project into shape.

Honestly, I'm not sure why a lot of the stuff we've learned here isn't taught in school. Demystifying gender differences and breaking down barriers (real and imagined) would go a long way toward creating a better world for all of us, and certainly, better relationships.

Happy Writing,
Jackson Dean Chase
Get a free book at
www.JacksonDeanChase.com

BIBLIOGRAPHY

FOR HOW TO WRITE REALISTIC WOMEN

FICTION

- *The Bitch Posse* by Martha O'Connor

NONFICTION

- *45 Master Characters* by Victoria Lynn Schmidt
- *Daring Greatly: How the Courage to Be Vulnerable Transforms the Way We Live, Love, Parent, and Lead* by Brené Brown
- *In the Mix: Struggle and Survival in a Women's Prison* by Barbara Owen
- *Queen Bees & Wannabes: Helping Your Daughter Survive Cliques, Gossip, Boyfriends, and the New Realities of Girl World* by Rosalind Wiseman
- *Reviving Ophelia: Saving the Selves of Adolescent Girls* by Mary Pipher, Ph.D.
- *The Virgin's Promise: Writing Stories of Feminine Creative, Spiritual, and Sexual Awakening* by Kim Hudson

- *The Writer's Journey: Mythic Structure for Writers* by Christopher Vogler

MEMOIR

- *Loose Girl: A Memoir of Promiscuity* by Kerry Cohen

TESTS AND ARTICLES (Google 'em!)

- Anatomy of the Female Anti-Hero by Lauren Duca
- The Bechdel Test
- 10 Ways to Spot A Manic Pixie Dream Girl
- The Mary Sue Test

WHAT'S NEXT?

NOW THAT YOU'VE MASTERED the basics of character creation, it's time to move on to more specific goals:

- *Writing Dynamite Story Hooks* walks you through how to emotionally hook readers step by step, line by line regardless of what genre you write.

- *Writing Monsters & Maniacs* covers a broad range of alien and fantasy races, killer robots and other machines, as well as all your favorite monsters and psycho killers. It includes 150 plot ideas plus tons of suggested movies and TV shows.

- *Writing Apocalypse & Survival* takes you into the apocalyptic and post-apocalyptic genres, giving you complete, infinitely expandable plot templates as well everything you need to know about what happens when the world ends. The book covers zombies, *Mad Max*-style road warriors, and more.

If you need help describing things—and I do mean anything—than be sure and grab my *Writers' Phrase Books*:

- #1 Horror
- #2 Post-Apocalypse
- #3 Action
- #4 Fantasy
- #5 Fiction (a short series sampler)
- #6 Science Fiction
- #7 Romance, Emotion, and Erotica

Note that the phrase books are intended as standalones, so all but the Romance one repeat a lot of the same action descriptions. You may not need to own more than one or two of these phrase books.

That's all till next time. Thank you for buying my book and I hope to see you again soon.

— Jackson Dean Chase
Get a free book at
www.JacksonDeanChase.com

P.S.: If you enjoyed this book, please leave a review to help others on their author journey.

ABOUT JACKSON DEAN CHASE

JACKSON DEAN CHASE is a USA TODAY bestselling author and award-winning poet. His fiction has been praised as "irresistible" in *Buzzfeed* and "diligently crafted" in *The Huffington Post*. Jackson's books on writing fiction have helped thousands of authors.

FROM THE AUTHOR: "I've always loved science fiction, fantasy, and horror, but it wasn't until I combined them with pulp thrillers and *noir* that I found my voice as an author. I want to leave my readers breathless, want them to feel the same desperate longing, the same hope and fear my heroes experience as they struggle not just to survive, but to become something more." — JDC

www.JacksonDeanChase.com
jackson@jacksondeanchase.com

BB bookbub.com/authors/jackson-dean-chase
g goodreads.com/Jackson_Dean_Chase
f facebook.com/jacksondeanchaseauthor
O instagram.com/jacksondeanchase
y twitter.com/Jackson_D_Chase

THE ULTIMATE AUTHOR'S GUIDE TO

WRITING
DYNAMITE
STORY HOOKS

A MASTERCLASS IN FICTION + MEMOIR

JACKSON DEAN CHASE
USA TODAY BESTSELLING AUTHOR

SNEAK PREVIEW OF WRITING DYNAMITE STORY HOOKS

INTRODUCTION

THE FIRST WORDS ON THE PAGE are the hardest you'll ever write. It's easy to get overwhelmed by choices. How do bestselling authors do it? That's what I set out to discover. I tore apart my library, scouring the openings to hundreds of my favorite novels and short stories to see what makes them work and why. And do you know what I found? A pattern—a secret formula authors use time and time again to deliver powerful, bestselling results. And do you know what else?

- *Genre doesn't matter.*
- *Point of view doesn't matter.*
- *It works for novels, novellas, and short stories.*
- *It works for series or standalone books.*
- *It even works for memoirs.*

So WHAT IS THE SECRET FORMULA?

The secret is in the story's opening line and how you construct it to "hook" readers into wanting more. A story hook is a literary technique that grabs readers' attention. Usually, the hook is in the first line, but sometimes it's in the second. More rarely, it only becomes evident after reading the first paragraph or two. It depends on the story the author is telling and what effect they're trying to achieve. The longer you delay your hook, the more likely readers are to stop reading, so never delay your hook longer than necessary!

The formula in this book will teach you how to write killer hooks —the kind that get noticed by agents, editors, and readers. My formula contains ten sure-fire ways successful authors use to open their stories and ten ways unsuccessful authors use.

Were there exceptions? Of course, but I quickly found the pattern and unlocked that secret formula too. I learned that in skilled hands, some of the wrong ways can actually be turned into the right ways (but it's tricky, and not always done the way you think).

In this breakthrough book, I'm going to reveal all these secrets and more in an unbeatable quick and dirty system that will take your writing to the next level. I break down how and why each way succeeds or fails with clear examples from bestselling fiction that show you how the formula works.

How to Write Dynamite Story Hooks is an easy to read, easy to use toolkit designed to be your "go to" guide every time you start a new story. Let's face it: in today's tough market, we all need an edge.

This book is the *secret weapon* you've been waiting for!

— JACKSON DEAN CHASE
Get a free book at
www.JacksonDeanChase.com

P.S.: "Fair Use" law prevents me from quoting more than roughly 300 or so words from another author's copyrighted material, so although I may quote from multiple books by the same author, I've been forced to limit how much I quote from any one source.

This sometimes results in me skipping over one or more paragraphs to get to the part that's most relevant to making my point. Whenever this occurs, I call it out in the text or use ellipses (…). Otherwise, even when broken up by my commentary, the scenes play out exactly as they do in the source material.

CHAPTER 1: SNEAK PREVIEW

ACTION

THE NUMBER ONE WAY to open a genre book is with action, but be careful how you set it up. You can't jump into a fight scene before you introduce your hero.[1] No one knows him, so no one cares what happens to him. So how do you do it?

Announce the action is taking place and place the enemy close, but not too close. This allows you to get your hero's reaction to the danger, providing valuable insight into who they are, where they are, and what they are up to when the action occurs:

> Logen plunged through the trees, bare feet slipping and sliding on the wet earth, the slush, the wet pine needles, breath rasping in his chest, blood thumping in his head.
>
> — JOE ABERCOMBIE, THE BLADE ITSELF

This is a prime example of how to open *in media res* (Latin for "in the middle of things"). Who is Logen? We know he's in a forest, struggling to escape, but from what? Let's see how bestselling grimdark fantasy author Joe Abercrombie handles it in his complete opening paragraph:

Logen plunged through the trees, bare feet slipping and sliding on the wet earth, the slush, the wet pine needles, breath rasping in his chest, blood thumping in his head. He stumbled and sprawled onto his side, nearly cut his chest open on his own axe, lay there panting, peering through the shadow forest.

We learn Logen has an axe, so whatever he's running from is more than he and his weapon can handle. We also pay off the potential danger of his "bare feet slipping and sliding" from the first sentence by making Logen fall in the second. That lets us know Logen is not invincible, nor is he immune to fear or accidents.

Abercrombie has efficiently *humanized* his hero right from the start by showing, not telling.[2] If he'd simply told us Logen was afraid, that would have been lazy writing. Instead, he shows us through internal and external sensory details. The fast, choppy style conveys panic. As a result, readers can empathize with Logen. The only problem is, we don't know much about him. That's where the second paragraph comes in:

The Dogman had been with him until a moment before, he was sure, but there wasn't any sign of him now. As for the others, there was no telling. Some leader, getting split up from the boys like that. He should've been trying to get back, but the Shanka were all around. He could feel them moving between the trees, his nose was full of the smell of them. Sounded as if there was some shouting somewhere on his left, fighting maybe. Logen crept slowly to his feet, trying to stay quiet. A twig snapped and he whipped around.

This second paragraph tells us everything else we need to know: Logen is the leader of a band of fighting men, and he has not willingly abandoned them, but been split off during a retreat from a superior force. This deepens reader empathy. The hero is not a coward, simply unlucky. Everyone can relate to that.

In the next few paragraphs, Logen is attacked by two of the Shanka and we see how well he fights. But the author does not let this happen before we get a sense of who his hero and his allies are, where they are, and what's going on. That is critical to the success of not only the book, but the author, and why he received reviews like, "You'd never guess that *The Blade Itself* is Joe Abercrombie's first novel. He writes like a natural."

The Blade Itself opens with the hero already in motion and the bad guys hot on his tail. Here's an example from a sci-fi perspective:

Death came for him through the trees.

— STEVE PERRY, THE MAN WHO NEVER MISSED

You can't get better than that. In a single, powerful sentence, we know the hero is in a forest and in terrible danger. From there, the author fills us in on what the danger is:

It came in the form of a tactical squad, four people walking three-and-one, the point followed by the tight concave arc; the optimum number in the safest configuration. It was often said the Confed's military was always training to fight the last war and it was true enough, only there had been enough last wars to give them sand or cold or jungle troops as needed. These four were jungle-trained, they wore class-one shiftsuits with viral/molecular computers able to match backgrounds within a quarter second; they carried .177 Parkers, short and brutal carbines which held five hundred rounds of explosive ammo—one man could put down a half-meter-thick tree with two waves of his weapon on automatic. The quad carried heat sensors, com-implants, Doppler gear and personal sidearms; they were the deadliest and best-equipped soldiers the Confed could field and they were good. They moved through the cool rain forest quietly and efficiently, alert for any signs of the Shanda Scum. If something moved, they were going to spike it, hard.

From the second paragraph[3], we know this is a sci-fi story, we know the "evil empire" is called the Confed, and they have been at war a long time. We also get a sense of the technology available to them and who they are hunting for (rebel scum). All good stuff, but we still don't know who the hero is. That's fine, because Steve Perry skillfully provides that information in the third paragraph:

> Khadaji felt the fear in himself, the familiar coldness in the pit of his belly, an old and unwelcome tenant. He had learned to live with it, it was necessary, but he was never comfortable when it came to this. He took a deeper breath and pressed his back harder against the rough bark of the sumwin tree. He practiced invisibility. The tree was three meters thick, they couldn't see him, and even without his confounder gear their directional doppler and heat sensors wouldn't read through that much solid wood. He listened as they moved past him. The soft ferns brushed against the shiftsuits of the quad; the humus of a thousand years made yet softer sounds under their slippers as they walked, but Khadaji knew exactly where they were when he stepped away from the tree.

You can guess what happens next: Khadaji assassinates the entire quad. After all, the name of the book is *The Man Who Never Missed*.

But what if you want to open with your hero *before* the bad guys are actively hunting her? This next example shows how to do that:

> The attack came in the hour before dawn. The girl woke to the stench of burning thatch and the sound of her mother screaming.[4] Outside, in the clearing beyond the hut, she heard her father's response, and the clash of iron on bronze. Another man shouted—not her father—and she was up, throwing off the hides, reaching back into the dark behind the sleeping place for her skinning knife or, better, her axe. She found neither. Her mother screamed again, differently. The girl scrabbled frantically, feeling the fire scorch her skin and the sliding ache of fear that was the threat of a sword-cut to the spine. Her fingers closed on a haft of worn wood, running down to the curve of a grip she knew from hours of oil and polish and the awe of youth; her father's boar spear. She jerked it free, turning and pulling the leather cover from the

blade in one move. A wash of predawn light hit her eyes as the door-skin was ripped from its hangings and replaced as rapidly by a shadow. The bulk of a body filled the doorway. Dawn light flicker-ed on a sword blade. Close by, her father screamed her name. *"Breaca!"*

— MANDA SCOTT, DREAMING THE EAGLE

In one paragraph, we know the setting is a primitive village under attack, the time, that the hero is a girl named Breaca who is familiar with weapons, and that she is in danger. Note that the enemy doesn't appear until near the end of the first paragraph. Just long enough to give us the details we need to know *before* the violence begins.

You can pull off the same effect in countless situations, even if you don't begin with action. For example, your hero could be about to play the winning hand in an illegal high-stakes poker game when armed robbers bust in and demand the money. That gives your opening the added advantage of misdirection. The reader thinks he's getting a scene about gambling, then you switch to robbery. The hero goes from winner to loser in a heartbeat, gaining reader empathy in the process.

Sometimes, stories begin with the hero witnessing violence without being involved.

We were about to give up and call it a night when somebody threw the girl off the bridge.

They came to a yelping stop overhead, out of sight, dumped her and took off.

It was a hot Monday night in June. With moon. It was past midnight and just past the tide change. A billion bugs were vectoring in on us as the wind began to die.

It seemed to be a very final way of busting up a romance.

— JOHN D. MACDONALD, DARKER THAN AMBER

There are a ton of questions raised by this intro:

1. Who is the girl?
2. Is she dead or alive?
3. Who threw her off the bridge?
4. *Why* did they throw her?
5. What were the hero and his friend about to give up before they saw the girl thrown from the bridge?

The arrival of enemies doesn't have to bring with it immediate violence. It can merely be the *threat* of violence, the intimidation, indignity, and humiliation enemies bring.

My used bookstore had been open for just about a month when the police showed up. I hadn't called them, of course; a black man has to think twice before calling the cops in Watts. They came to see me late that afternoon. Two well-built young men. One had dark hair and the other sported freckles.

The dark one wandered around the room, flipping through random books, looking, it seemed, for some kind of contraband.

"Where'd you get all these books, son?" the other cop asked, looking down on me.

I was sitting in my favorite swivel chair behind the makeshift table-desk that I used for book sales and purchases.

"Libraries," I replied.

"Stole 'em?" the dark-haired cop asked from across the room. There was an eager grin on his face.

— WALTER MOSLEY, FEARLESS JONES

There are no swords, no lasers, and nobody's dead (yet) but the threat is real. Menace hangs in the air: menace, bigotry, and hate. The cops are looking to roust the hero just because he's black, and maybe they're looking to do something more besides. A frightening situation, but a fantastic way to hook readers.

But what if it's not action with enemies, but with a natural disaster or some other dangerous survival situation? What do you do then? Pretty much the same thing:

I was thrown out of bed.

— RUDOLPH WURLITZER, QUAKE

It doesn't get simpler than that! The author isn't fooling around and has no intention of wasting our time. He just jumps right in, and that's fine because there's only the hero to focus on and a disaster he can't do anything about. The rest of the opening continues the danger:

The mirror fell off the wall and shattered over the dresser. The floor moved again and the ceiling sagged towards me.

The first paragraph establishes the bedroom and the danger. The second expands the setting and the action, as well as the strange, deadpan reaction the hero has. This tells us we're dealing with a potentially unreliable narrator.

It was dawn and I was in the Tropicana Motel in Los Angeles. There was another trembling through the room and what sounded like wires snapping and windows breaking. Then it was very quiet. I lay back on the floor and shut my eyes. I was in no hurry. There was a high prolonged scream by the pool and then a splash and another, shorter scream. I stood up and raised my arms over my head and tried to touch my toes, an early morning ritual I never perform. The wall next to the bed was moving as if it was alive and I walked into the bathroom.

Another kind of hero would react to in a different manner with the expected panic or bravery. But Wurlitzer isn't interested in normal. His hero does the opposite of what any sane person would do, and that's what makes him interesting. He doesn't care if he lives or dies. Maybe a post-quake world is better than the one before…

Comedy can also work with action to hook readers:

My sister threw down the book she was reading. To be exact, she threw it at me.

— ROBERT E. HOWARD, "THE LITTLE PEOPLE"

Thrown objects are funny, but what about thrown people?

They threw me off the hay truck about noon.

— JAMES M. CAIN, THE POSTMAN ALWAYS RINGS
TWICE

Action doesn't have to be violence or fast motion; it can be almost any criminal act:

He always shot up by TV light.

— JAMES ELLROY, AMERICAN TABLOID

Action can imply guilt (or protestations of innocence):

The building was on fire, and it wasn't my fault.

— JIM BUTCHER, BLOOD RITES

Action can show illness or injury:

As Roy Dillon stumbled out of the shop, his face was a sickish green, and each breath he drew was an incredible agony.

— JIM THOMPSON, THE GRIFTERS

Opening with someone hurt, sick, or dying creates sympathy and excitement. Readers become invested in the outcome and want to find out how it happened.

Action can also show surprise and instantly reveal genre:

I was staring out the classroom window when I spotted the flying saucer.

— ERNEST CLINE, ARMADA

Action can also represent a flurry of activity, even if centered around a seemingly normal event:

As the clock ticked down on her senior year in high school, Laurel McBane learned one indisputable fact.
Prom was hell.

— NORA ROBERTS, SAVOR THE MOMENT

Let's come full circle and end this chapter as it began—with violence, but not just any violence. The difference here is the violence is resolved *before* the first sentence:

After the guy was dead and the smell of his burning flesh was off the air, we all went down to the beach.

— STEPHEN KING, "NIGHT SURF"

What kind of sick weirdos would burn a guy to death then go party? If you want to find out, you have to read more, and Stephen King knows that. The rest of his paragraph neatly segues into casually talking about the narrator's friends—normal teenage stuff—but all is not as it seems and the narrator drops clues about a world-ending plague which means there was a good reason to burn that guy after all!

Other than shock value, the advantage to this opening is

combining action with mystery. Burning the body creates the action, while the follow-up creates the mystery. Which leads us to the first story secret:

STORY SECRET #1

COMBINING DIFFERENT OPENINGS

Combining different ways to open your story can create all kinds of interesting results. It's an advanced technique, but when you get it right, it's just as valid a way to open as any of the ten ways on their own—perhaps even more so.

Go back and look at the excerpts in this chapter. Notice they didn't just hook with action, but with mystery, like Stephen King did in "Night Surf." Who is Logen running from? What threw the narrator out of bed? Why is Roy Dillon sick? It's a one-two punch!

CHAPTER 1 FOOTNOTES

- 1 I define the word "hero" to mean any gender.
- 2 For more about why telling is a terrible way to open your novel, see Chapter 17: Telling or Info-Dumping.
- 3 This paragraph is a bit long, but gets the job done. Back when *The Man Who Never Missed* was written (1985), longer paragraphs hadn't gone out of fashion yet. If you write something like this now, I recommend breaking it up into shorter paragraphs.
- 4 A hero waking up is normally a bad way to open, but it works here because it's a reaction to danger.

That's it for this sneak preview. Want to learn nine more ways to successfully hook readers? Not to mention the ten ways that don't work? Buy *Writing Dynamite Story Hooks* today! And look for *Writing Monsters & Maniacs*, *Writing Apocalypse & Survival*, and my *Writers' Phrase Books* series which help you describe anything and everything!

SPECIAL FREE BOOK OFFER

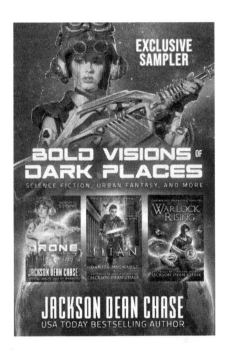

BOLDLY GO WHERE NO BOOK HAS GONE BEFORE

— FREE EXCLUSIVE SAMPLER —

"BOLD VISIONS of DARK PLACES"

featuring the best new sci-fi, urban fantasy, and more

by USA Today bestselling author Jackson Dean Chase

Get your free book now at

www.JacksonDeanChase.com

Made in the USA
San Bernardino, CA
25 July 2018